WHERE IS GOD IN SUFFERING?

where is god in suffering?
brendan purcell

VERITAS

Published 2016 by
Veritas Publications
7–8 Lower Abbey Street
Dublin 1
Ireland
publications@veritas.ie
www.veritas.ie

ISBN 978 1 84730 683 8

10 9 8 7 6 5 4 3 2 1

Extract from 'Aubade' by Philip Larkin, taken from *The Complete Poems*,
copyright © Philip Larkin. Published by Faber and Faber Ltd. Used with
permission.

Extracts from 'The Knockdown Question' by Les Murray, taken from *New
Collected Poems*, published by Carcanet, 2003. Reprinted by permission of
Carcanet.

A catalogue record for this book is available from the British Library.

Typeset by Padraig McCormack, Veritas Publications
Printed in Ireland by SPRINT-print Ltd, Dublin

*Veritas books are printed on paper made from the wood pulp of managed
forests. For every tree felled, at least one tree is planted, thereby renewing
natural resources.*

Contents

ACKNOWLEDGEMENTS

My first thanks are to Donna Doherty of Veritas – she's the one who had the idea for this book and encouraged me to write it after she'd heard me on Marian Finucane's programme responding to Stephen Fry. She's insightfully shepherded the text with her editor's version of the artist's genius in spotting what belongs and what's out of place or superfluous. I'd like to include here Donna's wonderful Veritas colleagues, Daragh Reddin and Emma O'Donoghue, who often understood better than I did what I was trying to say, and Lir Mac Cárthaigh, who never gave up looking for a suitable cover and found Georgia O'Keeffe's *Black Cross, New Mexico* to convey what can't be conveyed in words: while the Cross is a Christian symbol, it's plainly reaching beyond the horizon to become everyone's cross. O'Keeffe herself spoke of 'the feeling of infinity on the horizon line or just over the next hill,' and what's beautiful about Lir's choice is that beyond the wound of her Black Cross there's O'Keeffe's powerful evocation of the dawn of light and hope.

Secondly, I'm most grateful to RTÉ's Marian Finucane for asking me to respond to Stephen Fry's reason for rejecting God. Her incisive questions got me thinking more deeply about how suffering might be compatible with the existence of a good God.

I'm also grateful to Canon Dr Stephen Ames of Melbourne for inviting me to an earlier conversation with Professor Peter Singer in St Paul's Anglican Cathedral, to Bishop Brendan Leahy of Limerick for allowing me to draw on his wonderful sketch of Chiara Luce Badano's life, and to Dr John McNerney, who as Head Chaplain to University College Dublin gave me a home from home late last December as I worked over the book's first draft: thanks, John, for that and all the other great welcomes and discussions over the years.

Last Christmas over coffee in Milltown, Stephen Claffey woke me up from my dogmatic slumbers by clearly spelling out the more personal approach a book on suffering should take— thanks for that shock, Stephen! Always a luminous encourager, Professor David Walsh of Catholic University of America reminded me of Dostoevsky's relevance, as well as sharing with me his profoundly original philosophy of the person, however stumblingly it's communicated here.

My biggest thanks are to my incredibly generous friend Dr Joe McCarroll who, selfless scrivener that he is, patiently and penetratingly ploughed through the whole manuscript four times, gifted many of his philosophical, theological and scriptural insights (cheerfully adopted by this grateful author), suggested key references, while gently correcting howlers and clarifying obscurities – you're astounding, Joe!

I'm also very grateful to John Gaarlandt of Balans Press, Amsterdam and Board Member of the Etty Hillesum Foundation for kindly allowing me to quote so freely from her writings.

As ever, I'm most thankful to Archbishop of Dublin, Dermot Martin, who has kindly permitted me to work away in Sydney, to Archbishop of Sydney, Anthony Fisher OP, who since last Christmas has endured and is courageously overcoming the paralysis of Guillain-Barré syndrome, and to Cardinal George Pell, Prefect of the Secretariat of the Economy at the Vatican, who has lived through an unjust media and para-legal savaging with the difficult serenity of a John Fisher.

I'd like to dedicate this little book to three people who, despite my own spiritual deafness, more than anyone have taught me how to hear the voice of God in suffering—to the woman I've called **Darina** here, to **Marian Gilligan** (Eddie McCaffrey's great companion in suffering and in joy), and to **Vern Mulqueeney**, who asked the key question and is now living in the Answer.

ONE: INTRODUCTION
Listening to the voices of suffering

Recently, I've been considering those times during my seventy-four years on this planet when I experienced real suffering. One of the incidents that stands out involved having to part from someone I'd become very close to (I'll tell that story later on in the book), so that, on and off for years afterwards, I felt as though I'd been torn in two like a sheet of paper.

On another occasion, when I'd taken a sabbatical from teaching in order to do research at the wonderful University of Chicago, I experienced a moment of crippling existential doubt. I was slowly recovering from a broken leg during a typically snowbound Chicago winter; one night I was hobbling up and down the little day chapel on the ground floor of St Thomas Apostle rectory, where I was living, when I was seized by panic and, for just a few moments, I wondered: is there a God out there? Is there any meaning to what I'm doing? It took me a while to remember how another One had asked questions like these with his abject cry: 'My God, my God, why have you forsaken me?' A God-Man experienced himself a lot further from God and many of his closest companions on earth than I ever could, a double laceration of separation, from God and from human community. Just knowing I wasn't on my own in that crisis of meaninglessness, that he'd chosen to be there for me too, helped me join him in his huge act of trust – 'into Your hands' – and move beyond doubt in the company of the great Doubter.

And every one of us has had to go through the loss of friends and family members, or contend with feelings of helplessness at being unable to relieve another's suffering or support someone dear to us in their addiction. For others, there may have been the searing pain caused by the betrayal of someone they thought they could trust with their life.

Many of you will have had your lives turned upside down, your self-confidence and self-worth shaken, and your faith sorely challenged. If it was a really great suffering it may have prompted not just an anguished or angry shout of 'why, Lord?' but a why of prayer, a prayer of why.

When Stephen Fry, the English broadcaster and actor, was asked by Gay Byrne on *The Meaning of Life*, an RTÉ series exploring the spirituality of celebrity guests, what he'd say to God if he were passing through the pearly gates, as an entrenched atheist he gave a spirited denunciation of a God who allows the innocent to suffer. I'm grateful to him for his frank and eloquent statement, since surely he speaks for many, and the questions he raised are the ones I'll be discussing in this book. I'd like the book to be a continuation of that debate, though admittedly with fewer fireworks.

Archibald MacLeish was a well-known American writer, poet and dramatist during the middle years of the twentieth century. In *J. B.* (1958), his modern version of the Book of Job, one of his characters says: 'If God is good He is not God. If God is God He is not good.'[1] (He meant that a good God wouldn't allow suffering, but if there is a God, given there is suffering in the world he's created, he couldn't be good.) We'll see that Stephen Fry and Professor Peter Singer make a similar point, albeit rather less pithily.

This issue has been playing on my mind since receiving an invitation from one of Ireland's most experienced radio interviewers, Marian Finucane, to speak on her show and discuss Fry's comments.[2] Shortly after that, Donna Doherty at Veritas asked me if I'd expand what I'd said into a little book on suffering. You'll find the results in the following pages.

Suffering isn't something we can cure with theoretical discussion alone. Mircea Eliade, a world-famous philosopher of religion, tells the following story. At a soirée in Paris in the 1940s, a Romanian woman asked a well-known French philosopher about the meaning of evil. He gave the standard answer, insisting that it was the deprivation of a good. Unsatisfied by this rather intellectual reply, she later told Eliade, a fellow Romanian, about her husband, a priest who'd been brutally beaten to death by a prison guard for hearing another inmate's confession through the bars of his cell window. This guard, out of sheer malevolence, later turned up at the priest's funeral and – knowing full well she was aware who he was and what he'd done – gave her the traditional Romanian funeral offering of boiled wheat grains mingled with honey and nuts. That savage murder and the additional calculated insult had prompted her to ask about the meaning of evil.

Like the Romanian woman, if we're experiencing great suffering, a theoretical explanation is of little value. When speaking to young people in Nairobi on 27 November 2015, Pope Francis spoke words to the same effect:

> there are some questions that you can turn around in your minds over and over again and never find the answer to. 'How can I see the hand of God in one of life's tragedies?' I was going to say there's just one response but no, there's no response. There is a path.

I'm inviting you, the reader, to come along that path with me, conscious that I have no glib solution to offer, but also conscious that others who have travelled that path before us can help us along the way; perhaps they can lead us towards a few hilltops where we can see a little further ahead, if not beyond our suffering, at least towards a horizon from where it may become a little more bearable.[3]

Chapters One and Two will each take up three questions arising out of the Stephen Fry interview and my own public conversation with Professor Peter Singer in Melbourne in 2012, since these both help us to explore that statement: 'If God is good He is not God. If God is God He is not good.'

As Pope Francis said above, suffering is a path, something to be lived, not to be explained away. But even a wise pope like Francis has struggled to make sense of suffering, as evident in his response to seven-year-old William from the United States who asked him: 'If you could do one miracle, what would it be?' He answered, 'Dear William, I would heal children. I've never been able to understand why children suffer. It's a mystery to me. I don't have an explanation.'[4] Neither will anything here 'explain' suffering, but I hope that listening to the voices of others who have suffered may help us on our own way. Chapters Three to Six will explore other people's stories about how they managed to cope with suffering.

When I heard Stephen Fry saying bone cancer in children convinced him God could not exist, I immediately thought of the way Chiara Luce Badano, in her late teens, had turned to God in response to her own agonising struggle with that very disease. So in Chapter Three I'll explore her response to her illness. In Chapter Four, I'll consider the struggle of a young Dutch Jewish woman, Etty Hillesum, through her diaries and letters, as she tries to come to terms with life before and during her time in a Nazi concentration camp.

Newly appointed Auxiliary Bishop of Los Angeles, Robert Barron answered Fry's impassioned challenge to the existence of God, commenting wryly that 'the most devastating rant ever uttered against God' was not to be found in remarks like those of Stephen Fry, 'but rather in the pages of the Bible … the Book of Job'. He finds the best rejoinder to be 'a distinctively Christian one, for Christians refer to the day on which Jesus was unjustly condemned, abandoned by his friends, brutally scourged … nailed to an instrument of torture and left to die as "Good Friday". To understand that is to have the ultimate answer to Job …'[5] Following Bishop Barron's line of thought, in Chapter Five I'll consider how Job can become a voice that can enter into our own dialogue about suffering with ourselves and with God.

And, taking up Bishop Barron's second point, in Chapter Six, I'll come to what I think is the most profound experience of innocent suffering: Jesus' experience of crucifixion and 'forsakenness'. This, I believe, is a voice of suffering that everyone

– Christian and non-Christian, believer and non-believer alike –
can respond to.

The attacks on the US on 9/11 were quickly seized upon
by 'the four horsemen' of modern atheism: Richard Dawkins,
Christopher Hitchens, Sam Harris and Daniel Dennett. They
didn't blame Islamist terrorists, but all religions – Jewish,
Christian, Islamic and Hindu alike – for that horrific mass
murder (Buddhism generally got a pass). The afterword in
this book explores my own reaction at the time to 9/11, along
with how others, such as Pope Benedict XVI, Syrian Fr Jacques
Mourad, Rabbi Jonathan Sacks and moderate Muslims, have
responded to the question terrorism poses to believers.

If there's a common thread running through this little
book, it's that suffering is addressed to us as persons, and that
we – and those affected by it – may be somehow able to grow
as persons by the courage and love it demands of us. Perhaps
you don't immediately see your suffering in relation to God, but
isn't it often the way that when we have the privilege of sharing
time and conversation with those who are going through real
suffering, their courage and their words stay with us and change
the way we see things? So perhaps some of the experiences in
Chapters Three to Six may find an echo in your own.

TWO: VERN MULQUEENEY
'I think you got this one wrong, or did you?'

Vern Mulqueeney's question

Suffering is a mystery, isn't it, a bridge across our common humanity? Your suffering moves me, communicates itself to me wordlessly so I feel with you and for you. I feel something of what it'd be like to have to go through what you're going through. Call it what you like – solidarity, fellow-feeling, empathy, compassion – we undergo hard and terrible things and they pass from you to me, uniting us on the most primordial level of our shared humanness.

It's the mystery of our universal humanity. We're moved most by the suffering of those closest to us, but aren't we also affected by suffering in someone we don't know at all, someone we pass by in the street, sleeping in a doorway, on a night when it's wet, cold and windy? And aren't we moved, too, by images of those suffering brought to us by the media? As well as hurting us physically or emotionally, mentally, spiritually or religiously, real suffering often shocks and distresses us, affronts us, challenging everything we've built our lives on, evoking from us the anguished question: what does this suffering mean?

One of the greatest privileges I've had in my life is to have listened to the stories of those who have experienced great suffering.[6] I think of Vern Mulqueeney, a truckdriver who died in his forties having battled with multiple sclerosis for many years. A few years before, I'd met his amazing mother, Claire, while taking part in a TV discussion about euthanasia, where she maintained that she'd help her son to die if he were no longer able to breathe. Before the show I'd thought she wouldn't want to speak to me, but she came right over to me, we had a friendly chat, and after the programme she said she wouldn't ever help Vern to die, but had said otherwise to reassure him that she wouldn't watch him suffer.

I started visiting Vern every few months – Claire of course was with him every day. It got harder for Vern to speak, but he could tell me how he'd been trying to help others who suffered from severe disabilities in the care home where he lived. He greeted the news his young daughter was expecting a child with a poem, beginning, 'My baby's having a baby. Wow!' And that little infant brought huge joy into his life. When he still could, he'd sit out with the others in their wheelchairs and sometimes get them to laugh. He made up poems for them, my favourite being, 'Are you listening God?' which ends:

I know you are powerful, mighty and strong
but personally I think
you got this one wrong
or did you?

I never felt we needed to talk about God. Vern's 'Or did you?' said all that needed to be said.

Why this book was written

In addition to the aforementioned Stephen Fry[7] interview, which was viewed more than five million times just one week after being posted on YouTube, another source of inspiration for this book was a debate I was invited to in St Paul's Anglican Cathedral in Melbourne with the controversial philosopher Professor Peter Singer. The debate was on the subject: 'The Role of Reason in Faith and Unbelief.'[8] Singer's reason, in brief, for rejecting the existence of a 'good' God is the suffering of animals and innocent human beings. How could an all-powerful God, supposedly gifted with foreknowledge, allow such terrible events to happen?

Like Professor Singer, Stephen Fry roundly rejected any kind of God that would permit such suffering. From his own harshly interrupted life, Vern had addressed a similar question more gently to God, 'It seems like you made a mistake'. Keeping Singer's and Fry's responses in mind – shared surely by very many for the same reasons – I'll try to take up Vern's next line, 'Or did you?'

In this first chapter, I'll have a look at the different kinds of suffering there are – from natural disasters (which affect human beings and animals in all sorts of terrible ways) to animal suffering and then to the suffering children have to go through – whether through natural disasters, illness or the evil actions of adults. The following chapter will consider the suffering adults go through, beginning with their inevitable death. But aren't the worst sufferings – like the Holocaust – caused by our misuse of our own freedom? This will bring us to the mystery of evil, whether in others, in ourselves, or both. Since Peter Singer and Stephen Fry, like some other atheists of our time, regard all religions as a major factor in the world's evils, or at best, useless for dealing with suffering, that'll be our final topic in the second chapter.

Underlying the rejection of God is a rejection of nature

While many use the existence of human suffering as a reason for denying the existence of God, I think that denial masks another denial – a denial that we'll soon see embodied in Ivan, one of the Karamazov brothers, in Dostoevsky's last and greatest book *The Brothers Karamazov*. The novel is ostensibly a murder story: one of the Karamazov brothers, the illegitimate Smerdyakov, kills the father, Fyodor – but it's Dmitry, the most passionate of the Karamazov brothers, who's wrongly accused of the murder. The Russian Tsar was seen as the father of his people and a Dmitry Karakozov had attempted to assassinate Tsar Alexander II in 1866. So peering between the lines, a Russian reader would have understood a wider, political theme beyond the obvious one of the disintegration of the family – the assassination of the Tsar. And beyond that lay Dostoevsky's principal theme – contemporary nineteenth-century society's attempt to murder God.

In the novel, Ivan doesn't so much deny God as reject God's world. And underlying the denial of God by the two contemporary atheists, Stephen Fry and Peter Singer, is their refusal to accept nature as it is – whether it's the nature of the physical world, animal nature, or human nature.

Albert Camus, an open-minded atheist, for years struggled against the imaginary worlds dreamt up by utopian thinkers of left and right. Those dream worlds were perfectly summed up by the early-nineteenth-century thinker, Novalis, when he said: 'The world shall be as I wish it!'[9]

As the antidote to the idea of forcing human nature to be perfect, Camus proposes our consent to being. At the beginning of *The Rebel* (more accurately translated as *Man in Revolt*), his 1951 study of the revolutionary thinkers who want to change human nature by force, he writes: 'The analysis of revolt gives rise at least to the suspicion that there is a human nature, as the Greeks believed, and contrary to the postulates of contemporary thought.' And at the very end of his study he remarks that, 'They no longer believe in that which is, in the world and in living man ...'[10] He deeply affirms the real world, *what is*, and not the twentieth century's utopian nightmares.

In this chapter, I'll focus on three key points:

1. the refusal to accept the natural world as it is;
2. the refusal to accept animal nature as it is;
3. the refusal to accept a world in which children suffer.

In every case, this refusal leads to a refusal of the existence of God, and we'll of course consider that; however, I'm suggesting here that the original revolt is a revolt against what Camus called 'that which is, in the world and in living man'. Our second chapter will focus more explicitly on what follows from the reality of human freedom, the most important part of our humanity, that is, the suffering caused by the misuse of our freedom, both by others, but also by ourselves. I'll also ask whether religious belief is any help in any of the various types of suffering. We'll finish that chapter with a few thoughts on that most inescapable suffering – the inevitability of our death. Again, the question in the background will be: should God have created beings that could freely abuse their own and others' freedom and, in addition, are fated to die?

Thanksgiving as antidote to the rejection of reality

In the final chapter of his last book, *Autobiography*, G. K. Chesterton develops Camus' profound acceptance of reality into a more interpersonal response that one of his biographers called his 'grammar of gratitude'.[11] Chesterton provides an antidote to those various refusals of reality, which we'll explore for the remainder of this chapter and the next. He thought that those most worth seeking out were those who 'specialised in humility', who were neither pessimists considering that life was no good, nor optimists for whom life was all good, but those who could have 'a great deal of gratitude even for a very little good'.[12]

The people discussed in this book – Vern Mulqueeney, James MacMillan, Eddie McCaffrey, Chiara Luce Badano, Etty Hillesum, Job – all of them seem to have achieved, despite their suffering, a deep acceptance of 'what is,' and of the reality that lies beneath the 'what is', of their anguish. Each of them would no doubt relate to the inspiring words of Etty Hillesum, written in Westerbork concentration camp. Somehow they all heard a voice in the depths of their heart, calling them through their suffering to a place beyond it:

My life has become an uninterrupted dialogue with You, O God, one great dialogue. Sometimes when I stand in some corner of the camp, my feet planted on Your earth, my eyes raised toward Your heaven, tears sometimes run down my face, tears of deep emotion and gratitude.[13]

Would a good God permit natural disasters?

Professor Peter Singer certainly doesn't think so. Speaking of the 'vast amount of pain and suffering' in the world, he writes that 'if God is all-knowing' he knows this. And if God 'is all-powerful and all-good he could and would have created a world without so much suffering'. While for Professor Singer, it's 'more plausible to believe that the world was not created by any god', still, 'if … we insist on believing in divine creation, we are forced to admit that the God who made the world cannot be all-powerful and all good. He must be either evil or a bungler'.[14]

While these remarks refer to any kind of suffering, let's think first of all of the sufferings caused by earthquakes, tsunamis, volcanic eruptions and other natural disasters. I'm a world-expert in falling – I tripped and fell on a single step and broke my leg outside the University of Chicago's Harper Library. Shouldn't I be muttering about the divine bungler who was so thoughtless as to impose the law of gravity on the world? Physicists tell us that gravity is one of the four fundamental forces keeping our universe together. Should God suspend gravity every time a sentient being is in danger of suffering a fall? The universe we live in simply couldn't exist at all if it wasn't held together by gravity. And we couldn't exist either. Falling – and the risk of it – are just part of the human condition. Geologists tell us that forces like gravity are linked to the formation and movements of tectonic plates on our planet, with their related earthquakes and volcanoes. The best we can do to alleviate suffering and death resulting from this is to use more accurate seismological forecasting and improved architecture for life in areas where such events are most likely.

The more we understand about our many-layered cosmos, the more we grasp the interdependence between the astrophysical, chemical, biological, botanical, zoological and human levels of existence. All of the levels are interlinked: without the burning out of stars, there could be no carbon or rocky planets; without billions of years of algae transforming the atmosphere, nothing beyond bacteria and other single-celled organisms could live on earth.[15]

Here's what Peter Ward and Donald Brownlee have written about plate tectonics (whose shifting movements underlie earthquakes and tsunamis, experienced by us as disastrous events):

> Plate tectonics play at least three crucial roles in maintaining animal life: it promotes biological productivity; it promotes diversity (the hedge against mass extinction); and it helps maintain equable temperatures, a necessary requirement of animal life. It may be that plate tectonics is the central requirement for life on a planet and that it is necessary for keeping a world supplied with water.[16]

And on earthquakes, Guillermo Gonzalez and Jay W. Richards write:

> Most of us associate earthquakes with death and destruction, but ironically earthquakes are an inevitable outgrowth of geological

forces that are highly advantageous to life. Heat flowing outward from Earth's interior is the engine that drives mantle convection and, in turn, crustal motions. A tectonically active crust builds mountains, subducts old sea floor, and recycles the carbon dioxide in the atmosphere, all of which make Earth more habitable.[17]

Since it's beyond our intellectual pay grade to imagine a gravity-free universe, maybe some cosmic humility is in order, so that we don't expect God to suspend the law of gravity across the ninety-one billion light years dimension of our observable universe, along with what scientists are now telling us about how important plate tectonics are for keeping our planet habitable. One of the reasons natural disasters wreak such havoc on the less developed parts of the earth is because of inadequate infrastructure and emergency responses. While major disasters often call forth extremely generous aid from the developed world, more long-term approaches often founder because of political and economic attitudes that resist transformation. At least in our time it's becoming possible with early warning systems, if effectively maintained, to greatly lessen the death toll caused by tsunamis.

So, the believer or the philosopher can thank God for providing us with an astrophysical universe governed by its basic laws – without which, so far as scientists understand, it couldn't exist. Lying on my back in the University of Chicago Medical Center after my fall, I was asked to fill out an insurance claim according to university regulations. I demurred: 'sorry, I can only blame my own stupidity.' My failure to adapt to the laws of nature wasn't a reason for questioning God's existence, but for questioning my own carelessness. Believers don't say that because we suffer in disasters God doesn't exist. What we do ask is what our suffering means and how it may be reconciled with God's love.

I completely agree then with Peter Singer's questioning of whether natural disasters are compatible with a 'good' God. Nothing can take away the horror of, for example, the loss of more than two hundred and thirty thousand lives following the tsunami in the Indian Ocean on 26 December 2004. But reflection on the planetary significance of the movement of tectonic plates, along with practical efforts at mitigating their effects, rather than expecting God to miraculously break the laws of nature every time such events occur, is our meaningful response to God's love in gifting us this universe, along with our reason, expressed in scientific understanding and technology. It doesn't seem to make sense to blame God for creating a universe bound together by its four fundamental forces: gravitational, electromagnetic, and the strong and weak nuclear interactions.

Wouldn't a good God have prevented animals from suffering?

As regards animal suffering, you may remember the poignant scene in the documentary *The March of the Penguins* when the skua flew in to prey on the baby emperor penguins. The adult penguins don't make a move to protect their young since they're unable to fly – which is why they breed and raise their chicks after trekking up to one hundred and twenty kilometres from the coast. Skuas face their own problem of survival, and penguin young are an important food source for them. The only way to avoid this kind of suffering is to abolish all carnivorous animals – without seals and salmon on the menu, Alaskan bears could only eat animal conservationists! We couldn't have the range of land and marine animals we do if they weren't bound to each other as food resources. While we can and should do all we can to protect the well-being of living organisms within our ecosystem, it is impossible to abolish all suffering from the animal kingdom.

Certainly we should avoid any unnecessary animal suffering. I can largely agree with Professor Singer's campaign against animal cruelty without endorsing his endowing conscious animals with the equivalent of human rights while denying them to unborn or very young children.[18] If you've heard about Asperger's syndrome sufferer, Temple Grandin, or read her fascinating books, you'll know how her ability to picture animals' minds has enabled her to carry out magnificent work for the humane treatment of livestock.

But if Peter Singer and, I presume, Stephen Fry, accept the theory of evolution and its achievement in giving us a framework within which we can at least in part link all living things together, then they're surely bound to accept the inevitable suffering that accompanies that enormous biological galaxy of interactions between species at all levels of development.

When I appeared on *The Late Late Show* some years ago to discuss Richard Dawkins' essay collection *The Devil's Chaplain*, I mentioned how my mother, despite having had to leave school at fifteen, was very well self-educated. Her only respite from looking after her four unruly sons came while sitting down for a leisurely breakfast, good book in hand, after we had been bundled off to school. Being a good old-school Catholic, she had never actually read the Bible, but, over a few years, she got from Genesis to the Apocalypse. Her next book was Charles Darwin's *On the Origin of Species*, chosen simply because she had never read it and knew it was important. She saw no contradiction between an attempt at explaining how all living things were interconnected and that the whole process was created by God.[19]

So if there are laws governing plant and animal growth, occasional breakdowns of these growth processes – cancer, for example – are statistically always likely to occur in biologically-based living beings. Animal pathologies that surely cause pain would seem to be an inevitable consequence of their being endowed with sensation. Anaesthetics prevent a person from feeling pain, and medicine may cure disease. But suffering and pain often warn us about underlying illness and so, in those natural instances at least, are good. What's needed is an examination of the different kinds of suffering.

We shouldn't expect God to suspend the evolutionary developmental laws underlying all living things in order to prevent disease in plants, animals and humans, any more than he should suspend the law of gravity binding the physical universe together to prevent tectonic plates from colliding. If he did, the K-T (Cretaceous-Tertiary) mass extinction of three quarters of all animal and plant species on Earth sixty-six million years ago leading to the mammal and marsupial development (including ourselves, much later) that replaced the dinosaurs, mightn't have happened. So the catastrophic asteroid strike on the coast of Yucatán, Mexico, blasting out the giant Chicxulub crater that caused the K-T event, was an important condition for the later enormous plant and mammal developments in the story of evolution.

Would a good God allow children to suffer?

As I've said, in the aforementioned *Meaning of Life* interview, Gay Byrne asked Stephen Fry if, supposing there were an afterlife, what would he say to God? Fry replied: 'I'll say, "Bone cancer in children? What's that about?" How dare you? How dare you create a world in which there is such misery that is not our fault? It's not right. It's utterly, utterly evil.'[20]

I'll let a teenager who died from bone cancer, Chiara Luce Badano, provide a rather different view to Fry's in our next chapter. But there's another question that such illnesses ask of us: what are we doing about it? Given that various grave illnesses are inevitable in our world, it's those, out of their great desire to help such children, who put their shoulder to the wheel, who have the strongest right to talk about and be heard on such issues. Journalist Damian Thompson, writing of the Scottish composer James MacMillan and his family, speaks on behalf of people who've actually done this:

> James and Lynne's daughter, Catherine, had a severely disabled daughter, Sara. Helping Catherine care for Sara was the private but overwhelming priority for Sir James and Lady MacMillan (as they now are) for the best part of six years. Sara's death in the first week of 2016 was unexpected and devastating. At her Requiem Mass, James gave a eulogy that celebrated Sara's life as a gift; he also deplored the fact that, in twenty-first-century Britain, there are 'caring' people who feel that a human being as physically broken as his granddaughter should not exist.[21]

Perhaps the mystery is that we see everything differently when we hear God calling us through our suffering. At any rate, between those who believe God doesn't exist and those who believe they're living their lives in an ongoing encounter with God – experiencing their sufferings in this Presence[22] – there's a big difference in how they see the meaning and importance of suffering. So I'll include here MacMillan's very recent, equally impassioned, words, because they provide a contrasting voice on the same question. MacMillan's eulogy communicates a kind of answer to Stephen Fry's question, the answer of a family responding to the need for love with more love. I think you'll see a profound harmony here between the voice of the MacMillan family and the other voices we'll be listening to in the following chapters.

Sir James MacMillan: Rapture gazing at rapture …

People say … that God intervened in human history. That is, he interfered with our story, to become one of us, to know what it means to be human, and for us to know Him and to discover that He loves us, with all the implications that has.

Other people will also maintain that this interference in our lives has manifested itself in other ways, perhaps less dramatic, less cosmic, less strange and inexplicable but with parallel revelations.

I can think of a few of these revelatory interferences … The music of J. S. Bach, the writings of Shakespeare, Michelangelo's *Pietà*, the evolution of democracy from ancient Greece to the fall of the Berlin Wall, Einstein's development of the Theory of Relativity … Celtic winning the European Cup in 1967.

Nearly six years ago my daughter Catherine gave birth to a beautiful little girl, Sara Maria, who was multiply handicapped due to Dandy Walker Syndrome. She had lots of problems, was helpless in every way, but she changed our world. She died on 5 January.

Over these years with Sara some of us experienced other, more gradual, more surprising, more silent and transformative realisations of the divine love I mentioned above in the unassuming, patient, tiny, broken, handicapped, smiling, listening, quacking, delighted presence of Sara.

It is not an exaggeration to say that lives have been changed through knowing this little angel; from her mother Catherine, whose life changed forever when she said yes to new life, to the wider family and friends who saw in this relationship an astonishing love and devotion, who saw rapture gazing at rapture, who saw tenderness embrace tenderness, who saw devotion build upon devotion, who saw worship meet worship, who saw the cherisher lift up the cherished, who saw the enchanter astonish the enchanted, who saw heart lost to heart. And how this deep and cosmic love spread out to everyone who was privileged to enter their lives. There are people throughout the world who have become different people through their associations with Sara ...

It is strange that this momentous interference in our stories has come from someone so weak and small. Our world celebrates strength and power, after all. We glorify in might and wealth and health and success. We cheer winners and achievers. We bow before men and women of financial clout. We laud politicians of guile and ruthlessness – the more rabble-rousing and populist the better these days, it seems.

Sara had nothing of any of this. Our society doesn't know what to make of children like Sara any more. There are some very important, powerful, professional, 'caring' people who made it clear that they thought Sara should not exist – that the compassionate response to her significant disabilities would be to stop her living, for her mother to say 'no' instead of 'yes' to Sara … Well, Sara interfered with that narrative, too, and turned it on its head.

Love itself, which is the fundamental necessity for human life and is the true signifier of the sanctity of life, is hard. It is easier to turn our backs on love. That is why these interferences I mention, whether they are from God, or Mozart or from wee Sara, are such blessings and transformations. We have been blessed and transformed through knowing and loving Sara, and being known and loved in return by her …

I pray that her divine interference, which has been her commission from God, will continue in unexpected ways in our lives, that our grief at her departure can be swallowed by the joy of remembering her and that we will join her again, one day, in heaven.[23]

Dostoevsky and the suffering of children

The main force of Stephen Fry's tirade against God is the suffering of children, causing him to reject a God who would permit this. While he only mentioned suffering due to natural causes, far more horrendous and difficult to understand is the suffering caused by evil adults. Fry's great refusal of God reminded me of a similar great refusal in Dostoevsky's masterpiece, *The Brothers Karamazov* completed in 1880, the year before he died. That refusal occurs when one of those brothers, Ivan Karamazov, rejects a world where children suffer terribly.

In this particular instance, Dostoevsky drew on contemporary news reports of actual cases where children had been tortured and murdered, as we could still do today. For example, Ivan tells of the story of educated parents who (all because she'd soiled her bed) flogged and kicked their five-year-old daughter and locked her in a cold dark outhouse all night, ignoring her weeping for 'dear God' to protect her. Or of the young serf who accidently injured the paw of the general's favourite hunting dog. The general had him locked up until morning, then stripped naked, before a pack of dogs tore him to pieces. From these horrific incidents, Dostoevsky has Ivan draw a conclusion – more forceful than Fry's rhetorical flourish – that if such suffering is required for the sake of universal harmony, 'I don't want harmony, for love of mankind, I don't want it … It's not that I don't accept God, Alyosha, I just most respectfully return him my ticket.'[24]

We'll be returning to Dostoevsky in our next chapter, but it's enough here to make the obvious point: that these events of terrible cruelty are caused by the evil actions of people, not by God. Certainly no orthodox Christian thinker ever considered the world as being in some kind of 'harmony', where the suffering of innocents was somehow balanced by the greater good of that harmony – whatever that greater good might be. For Christians, from the beginning, the order of the world has been profoundly disturbed due to the evil actions of human beings. This begins with Adam and Eve, then through the various cheerfully sinning Kings of Israel, on to Judas Iscariot – along with the one who formulated what I'd call 'the Caiaphas Principle' – that 'it is expedient for you that one [good] man should die for the people … that the whole nation should not perish' (Jn 11:50). The suffering of innocents (including the Holy Innocents massacred by Herod), while horrendous in itself, is directly caused by the evil deeds and characters of the adults who perpetrate them.

What's wrong with Ivan's diagnosis is that he fails to unearth the cause of such shocking events. Of course they're appalling, but we have to dig deeper to understand the essence of their evil, which is even worse than the emotional and physical suffering undergone by the children. At its dark heart is the perpetrators' deliberate attempt at radically depersonalizing others. As the Second Vatican Council diagnoses it, evil actions 'debase the perpetrators more than the victims' (*Gaudium et Spes*, 27). In *Notes from Underground*, Dostoevsky's Underground Man sees all relationships to others as using and abusing them:

> [W]ith me loving meant tyrannizing and showing my moral superiority. I have never in my life been able to imagine any other sort of love, and have nowadays come to the point of sometimes thinking that love really consists in the right – freely given by the beloved object – to tyrannize over her.[25]

Or as the philosopher Martin Buber puts it in his reflection on Napoleon (which is of course applicable to all who dehumanise others):

> He was for millions the demonic Thou, the Thou that ... responds to Thou with It ... This demonic Thou, to which no one can become Thou, is the elementary barrier of history ...He sees the beings around him, indeed, as machines ... which must be ... utilised for the Cause.[26]

All serious exploration of evil must begin with a self-examination of our own capacity for the wilful undoing of ourselves and others.

Flannery O'Connor on the suffering of children

American writer Flannery O'Connor wrote a challenging introduction to the story of the life of a girl called Mary Ann Long, born with a facial disfigurement, who died at twelve, but whose lively, joyful and mischievous spirit had inspired those who shared her life. Taking up the very accusation of God that Ivan Karamazov makes because of the suffering of little children, O'Connor focuses on the dangers inherent in Ivan's false primacy of feeling over morality – highly relevant for Stephen Fry's similar elevation of feeling into his principal reason for rejecting God:

> One of the tendencies of our age is to use the suffering of children to discredit the goodness of God, and once you have discredited his goodness, you are done with him … Busy cutting down human imperfection, they are making headway also on the raw material of good. Ivan Karamazov cannot believe, as long as one child is in torment; Camus' hero cannot accept the divinity of Christ, because of the massacre of the innocents. In this popular pity, we mark our gain in sensibility and our loss in vision. If other ages felt less, they saw more, even though they saw with the blind, prophetical, unsentimental eye of acceptance, which is to say, of faith. In the absence of this faith now, we govern by tenderness. It is a tenderness which, long since cut off from the person of Christ, is wrapped in theory. When tenderness is detached from the source of tenderness, its logical outcome is terror. It ends in forced labour camps and in the fumes of the gas chamber.[27]

Flannery O'Connor is criticizing what other writers diagnosed as *The Triumph of the Therapeutic* and *The Culture of Narcissism* – making our feelings the only standard for moral judgment. So we're prepared to kill people whose 'quality of life' we feel is not up to scratch, like gravely disabled infants, or adults suffering from serious mental incapacity. That reduction to feeling as the primary moral category was carried out, for example, by the French Enlightenment thinker Rousseau, who wrote in his 1762 novel, *Emile,* that 'to exist is to feel'. Horrendous as the suffering of children is, even worse is the moral evil of those adults who cause that suffering. Just as Ivan Karamazov and Stephen Fry are rightly appalled at that innocent suffering, should they not be even more appalled at the desecration of the image of God in those children by those who are dehumanised and dehumanizing? Our next chapter will try to continue this discussion of an evil not caused by God but by our fellow humans.

THREE: VIKTOR FRANKL
'Saying yes to life in spite of everything'

We'll continue with our thoughts on God and suffering, focusing here on the reality of human nature and its gift of freedom, and with the inevitable consequence that we're free to love and free not to love – a consequence traditionally spelled out dramatically by Cain's murder of his innocent brother, Abel. We'll first explore this awful implication of our freedom, then ask whether having a context of faith can hinder rather than help our freedom, and finally we'll touch on that unavoidable suffering every one of us – saint or sinner, billionaire or pauper – will have to undergo.

Does God cause evil?

I'd like to reword that question: if God creates us free, and we do wrong and hurt others, isn't it His fault? This brings us face to face with a mystery – why did God create us morally free in this way, what was His purpose? Let me draw on two different experiences:

First, in the early 1970s I was invited to a meal with a young couple in Brussels. They'd decided never to have children because of the danger of a nuclear war. I remember saying to them that the risk they'd be taking if they had a child wasn't unlike the risk God takes in creating us – the risk that it's better we exist with the enormous gift of our freedom, even though, as a result, we're also free to refuse to love (our discussion of the Book of Job later will develop this issue).

Second, 1968 wasn't only a year of student revolt in Paris, Berkeley, and elsewhere. In Italy, where family bonds were very close, students not only revolted against what they felt was political or cultural oppression, but against their parents. A friend of mine told me how this worked out in her own Milanese family, where her younger sister (I'll call her Marta here) had joined a far-left commune that had organised a pro-abortion demonstration inside Milan's world-famous Duomo. Complicating the situation were attacks by armed right-wing groups on communes like Marta's. Naturally, Marta's parents were deeply concerned for her and, living out their own commitment to the Gospel, they made sure she was always welcome at home. Among her group, Marta's were almost the only parents still in touch with their child – so she was always able to have her washing done at home and to carry on a dialogue with her parents.

One time she asked her father what he thought of what she was doing. He restrained himself from saying how much he wanted her to leave her group. Instead, he focused on what had been her ideal as a teenager in the youth branch of the Focolare Movement, saying: 'if you're sure that what you're doing is out of self-sacrificing love for the other, then keep on doing it.' She thought about that, and returned to her group. But a year or so later, realising the group's leaders were more keen on developing a political profile for themselves than on helping others, as well as misappropriating funds, Marta, remembering what her father had said, left the group.

I'd like to use the experience of Marta's father, and that of any parent, to illustrate God's role in creating us as free persons. Parents face situations like this all the time. We don't – we can't – determine what other people will do. Parents can advise, direct, train, warn, threaten and punish their children, but in the end, each person is free. This means they may know what they should do, yet freely choose not to do it – causing suffering for others.

Aquinas explores this question in his *Summa Theologica*, concluding that: 'God … neither wills evil to be done, nor wills it not to be done, but wills to permit evil to be done; and this is a good.'[28] The basic point is that what God wishes must happen, what he decides against cannot happen. But he can permit – that is not cause, but allow to happen – the good of being free persons, which implies we can use our freedom any way we want. This is what Marta's father did; he took the risk of allowing Marta to use her own freedom, even if that could lead to her moral or physical destruction. The Brussels couple were more like a God who decided that endowing human beings with freedom was too risky, that it'd be better to keep all animate beings at the level of the inhabitants of Dublin Zoo.

Let's see if Dostoevsky's more dramatic exploration of this question can help here.

Dostoevsky's Grand Inquisitor in *The Brothers Karamazov*

We've already considered the 'Rebellion' section of Dostoevsky's *The Brothers Karamazov* where Ivan Karamazov rejects a world in which God allows children to be tortured and killed. What follows is the single most famous section in all of Dostoevsky's writings, 'The Grand Inquisitor'. This section illuminates Dostoevsky's understanding of the mystery of human participation in evil.

There, in the tale made up by unbelieving Ivan, Christ is once again brought to trial, this time not before the Sanhedrin or Pilate but before the Grand Inquisitor as Prosecutor in sixteenth-century Seville. The reason the Grand Inquisitor sentences Christ to death is that Christ has endowed humankind with the gift of freedom, which Ivan and the Grand Inquisitor argue is far too high a responsibility for humans to bear. In refusing Satan's temptation of bread – 'man does not live by bread alone' – Christ has missed the point. Bread is what these contemptible humans are really after, not freedom, and they'll do all they can to find someone who'll take its burdens from them in exchange for bread.

Several times the Grand Inquisitor tells the silent Christ that 'we corrected your deed'. That correction has been achieved by reducing the masses to the level of bleating animals. It's a particularly prescient observation given the horrors visited on Russia by Lenin and the Bolsheviks in the twentieth century, where the hundreds of thousands of party elite shouldered the burden of freedom for the hundreds of millions of sheeplike masses.

Commenting on the Grand Inquisitor sequence, political philosopher David Walsh writes: 'He has rendered men less than human out of love for them but in the process has deprived them of all that makes them loveable'. Walsh goes on to note that freedom is that dimension of unlimited openness that enables us to go beyond all material limits. It's an awareness that we should choose death rather than compromise our freedom, which twenty-one-year-old Sophie Scholl showed in non-violently challenging the might of the Third Reich in 1943. Before leaving for her execution she scribbled the word 'Freedom' on the legal indictment she left in her cell.[29] Walsh notes how the great Dostoevsky interpreter Konstantin Mochulsky understood the deeper significance of Dostoevsky's 'Legend' when he said, 'without freedom, man is a beast, mankind, a herd', and saw that under Ivan's 'false compassion for the sufferings of mankind is hidden a diabolic hatred of human freedom and the "image of God" in man'.[30]

What Dostoevsky was showing – rather than arguing – was that it's not God who is responsible for the cruel mistreatment of children, but human beings like ourselves, who somehow would prefer not to rise to the level of their own responsibility. Their 'bread' is in fact their indulging in their own passions – whether for power, domination, sexual or other satisfactions – all of them below the level of free choice, grounded in a responsible commitment to achieving what is morally good.

In other words, God accepts the laws he has built into nature at its various levels. So we're confronted with the grandeur and tragedy of a creature whose freedom God utterly respects, even to the point of permitting those creatures to freely reject him, and as Mochulsky has pointed out, to desecrate the divine image in our fellow humans. The murder of God and the murder of humans are more closely connected, perhaps, than we realize. As

Eric Voegelin puts it, speaking of the Western cultural collapse that facilitated the emergence of Nazism, 'One cannot dedivinize [that is, remove God from] oneself without dehumanizing oneself – with all the consequences of dehumanization that we shall … have to deal with.'[31] Does this mean that the suffering and injustice inflicted upon our fellow human beings arises because we are bullied and misled by powerful evildoers? We have to accept that we too may be responsible for how we respond to such treatment.

Our own potential for evil

To help us focus on the problem, let's recall a comment from Aleksandr Solzhenitsyn in his book *The Gulag Archipelago*, warning against simply blaming Stalin or the KGB for the atrocities visited on his people: 'If only it were so simple! If only there were evil people somewhere insidiously committing evil deeds, and it were necessary only to separate them from the rest of us and destroy them. But the line dividing good and evil cuts through the heart of every human being.'[32] Or as David Walsh has put it:

> Failure to acknowledge that holocausts are not primarily external phenomena, but first exist as a possibility within each of us, has been the principal reason why we have still not been able to clarify the enormity of our recent modern past.[33]

And in the Marian Finucane interview I've already referred to, I mentioned secular Jewish philosopher Hannah Arendt's warning in *Eichmann in Jerusalem* – her 1963 report of the trial and sentencing to death of one of the principal Nazi facilitators of the Holocaust, Adolf Eichmann – against indulging:

> in sweeping statements about the evil nature of the human race, about original sin, about innate human 'aggressiveness,' etc., in general – and about the German national character in particular ... [But] in any event, one thing is sure, and this one had not dared to believe any more – namely, that everyone could decide for himself to be either good or evil in Auschwitz ... And this decision depended in no way on being a Jew or a Pole or a German; nor did it even depend on being a member of the SS.[34]

What these philosophers are saying is that the core of the problem of evil lies within the heart of each human being – that we're not only able to know what we ought to do, but that we're morally free to do it or not.

In my discussion with Marian Finucane, I developed this a little further, when I said that 'if God wants to have a creature which is free, God has to accept that freedom means freedom to reject him'. I would put this more positively now, and remind myself of our astonishment and delight when we discover ourselves to be morally free. But there is also our horror when we find we've freely chosen to do wrong, and our additional horror that we've wrought unfolding moral and physical wrongs, along with our dread at noticing that we've become disoriented and disordered by our freely chosen wrongdoing. Then we're enmeshed in a rollercoaster of freely chosen wrongdoing, deformed by the effects of our own or other's wrongdoing. Saint Paul, in the seventh chapter of his Letter to the Romans, spells out our universal experience of not doing the good we want to do, and doing the evil we don't fully want to do, along with our amazed thankfulness when we find our only hope is to be swept up into God's salvation, gifting us its many-levelled repairs and renewals. In this spiritual struggle we see how the terrible evils of our time come from freedoms misused and not from an inexplicably impotent or evil God.

When Marian Finucane referred to 'the potential within all human beings to do unspeakable things', I agreed: 'Absolutely. I think that's a really important point, Marian: the Holocaust is within me, it's not just something [others do]. We're all free, we can't simply blame the fact that we're under this ideology or that. And unfortunately, some of us, when we get the chance, we take it.' Another German Jewish philosopher, Hans Jonas, in his concluding remarks to his book, *The Concept of God after Auschwitz*, comes to mind. Jonas contrasts himself to Job, who 'invokes the fullness of the divine creative power, while mine is the renunciation of that power. And still – strange to say – both are praise: since renunciation is what makes it possible for us to be. This too, it seems to me, is a reply to Job: to know that in him, God himself suffers'.[35] I'll try to develop that enigmatic remark of Jonas in all of the chapters that follow.

What's the use of religious belief in suffering?

Professor Peter Singer opened the conversation we had in St Paul's Cathedral in Melbourne by referring to an article by a mathematician, William Clifford, called 'The Ethics of Belief'.[36] Clifford takes the example of a shipowner whose ship is carrying emigrants to seek their fortune elsewhere. His ship is rather old, and the owner is asked if it needs to be inspected to see if it's seaworthy. He replies that because he has faith in God, who wouldn't allow these good people with their babies to drown, his ship will make a safe voyage. In fact, the ship sinks, and all drown. Clifford says the owner wasn't justified because his faith wasn't justified, a faith contrary to the evidence.

Professor Singer presumed that what Clifford called faith in that example is normal in religion. For him, it wouldn't matter if it was simply a personal issue, but, as with the shipowner, when it impacts on the wider public, its effects can be disastrous. In Clifford's essay, he formulates as a basic principle that 'it is wrong always, everywhere, and for anyone, to believe anything upon insufficient evidence'. But what Clifford and Singer regard as the shipowner's faith is rather obviously culpable self-deception – it's interesting that Clifford had to make up an unbelievable fictional story of a character of nearly certifiable idiocy to illustrate what he called 'faith'.

While we don't have room here to look at what faith really means for a believer, Christian faith strangely passes one of Clifford's own tests for an acceptable faith at the end of his essay: 'We may believe the statement of another person, when there is reasonable ground for supposing that he knows the matter of which he speaks, and that he is speaking the truth so far as he knows it'. So the faith of a believer is never a blind faith, but rather a reliance on evidence, where that evidence includes trust in the one giving grounds for faith.

But what use is such a genuine religious faith? In his interview with Gay Byrne, Stephen Fry said that, 'The moment you banish [God] your life becomes simpler, purer, cleaner, more worth living in my opinion.' But, as I noted in an article just after that interview, it doesn't:

Firstly, not one of the problems, sufferings, tragedies and disasters that Fry would like to blame on God, goes away. Even worse, as Dmitry Karamazov says (in *The Brothers Karamazov*[37]), 'without God ... everything is permitted'. So when Lenin, Stalin, Hitler, Mao, Enver Hoxha and Pol Pot 'banished God', they banished a good few million human beings too.[38]

And in my interview with Marian Finucane, I said that:

[H]e's left with the same problems he was talking about right through the interview. In other words, would the world get any better if there's no God there? We've still got the problem of evil, of suffering ... What I'm saying is that these things don't go away: whether there's a God or not, everyone has to go through [testing experiences] – for example, you lose someone very close to you; you have an illness that's going to knock you out in a hurry. You find [suffering] in Judaism, in the Greek material, in Buddhism, Hinduism, they've all got different ways of [asking] 'how do we do something about suffering?' How do we somehow go beyond it? And, for me the biggest way, the Christian way is that God comes down and shares the pain with us. He doesn't give a quick answer, we go through it with Him – there's no quick answer, no quick fix.

To finish this chapter, here is an example of someone whose faith certainly made a huge difference to his life and the lives of many who came to know him.

EDDIE MCCAFFREY
'Able not to be able'

One of the first people who taught me so much about suffering was Eddie McCaffrey, born in Liverpool in 1949. When he was three or four, his mother, Margaret, noticed something wrong with his legs. He was diagnosed as suffering from muscular dystrophy, and his mother and his stepfather John were told there was no cure: 'you can't expect him to live out his teens'.

Eddie loved sports, so he suffered a lot at school, realising he could never play freely like the rest of his classmates. When he was about seven years old, Margaret remembered one time in particular when he asked her: 'Mum, do you mind having a boy like me?' She answered that when he was being created, God knew exactly how he'd be, and searched the Earth to find the mother who'd be exactly right for him. This explanation really pleased him, and Margaret thanked the Mother of God in her heart for giving her the right words when Eddie needed them.

When Eddie was seventeen he moved to Dublin, where he hoped to start university. While he passed the exams he studied for, he didn't get enough points to do the course he wanted. Overcome by emotional turmoil and believing his life to be without purpose, he no longer went to Sunday Mass. He was now nineteen. Margaret couldn't answer his questions, and felt he'd never get over his suffering, both physical and existential.

However, a friend named Tom Sherrard called by, and told Eddie about a way of living based on the Gospel, inviting him to an ecumenical meeting in Rome. The theme of the meeting was 'God is Love'. What impressed Eddie was that this theme was actually being lived by the men he was staying with there. When he told them he was used to sleeping with a board under his mattress, they took a door off a cupboard for his bed so he could sleep properly. When the group had an audience with the pope, Eddie, because he was in a wheelchair, was placed in the front row at St Peter's Basilica. He was really won over when Pope Paul VI came over to him, gave him a Rosary, and encouraged him to 'be patient and keep joy in your heart'.

The following day, when the group went to the Catacombs for Mass, everyone was astonished to find that the narrow passages were just wide enough to accommodate his wheelchair, with inches to spare. Eddie laughed: 'The first Christians must have known we were coming.' Back in Dublin, many young people began to call on him, and he got to know Marian, a neighbour, who'd recently been diagnosed with muscular dystrophy too. They became great friends, and composed words and music for songs together, which, since she could play the guitar, they could sing together with their friends.

The warm welcome he gave me the first time I shook his hand underlined for me the truth of the saying: see the person, not the disability. As a result of being one of those people who count for little in terms of the grasping and competitive world around him, he didn't intimidate people lacking in self-esteem.

'Kevin' (not his real name) was a profoundly depressed student I introduced to Eddie. They became friends and, as a result, Kevin was able to see his own true value, eventually passing his final exams after eight years of failure. Eddie said of Kevin early on, 'it's a pity he doesn't realise that you don't solve problems, you love them' – at least that's what Eddie had learned for himself. There was no cure for his own muscular dystrophy and no treatment at that time, but he'd somehow transcended his own suffering and learned not merely to accept but to love his incapacity. He had somehow learned to see a Christian meaning in this suffering, a subject that I'll explore in Chapter Six.

As he said to some of his friends, 'I can't give anything, the only way I can love is to receive, to be open to others.' After Eddie died, we found a copy of a poem he'd written for a young neighbour who, despite suffering from severe curvature of the spine, had managed to learn to ride a bike. It was called 'Courage on a Bicycle'. He didn't give much thought to his own courage, but wanted to affirm and celebrate that of another.

An elderly Redemptorist priest introduced some people with psychological problems to Eddie, in the hope that the encounter would help them put their own problems into perspective. Eddie's bemused response was, 'He thinks I'm a blinking shrine!' At night, when Margaret had put him to bed – she needed a hoist for this – he'd sometimes ask her to move him, saying, 'I'm still in an uncomfortable position.' He told us, 'put that on my tombstone: Here lies Eddie McCaffrey: He's still in an uncomfortable position!'

Towards the end of November 1979, now thirty, Eddie's health was deteriorating rapidly. Someone asked him at that time how he was: 'Fine. I lose strength every day, but who needs strength?' In those last weeks, he could hardly hold a pencil, but he asked Margaret for something to write with, and began a letter to Our Lady. He only lived a few days more, then passed away quietly in his sleep.

What can I say to you? Words seem only to spoil everything because your life speaks for itself. Why am I writing to you? I cannot answer even that ... I write to you because I am helpless and each day I am getting a little more so. Not only can I not do anything but I feel I am becoming nothing. I know you are not surprised to receive this letter because who else could I write to about nothingness but the expert on nothingness yourself?

… I want to tell you that I am happy to be nothing because it gives me the opportunity to be a little like you, who in your lowliness chose the hidden way with a 'Yes' the world has never heard and will never hear again. What else could I be but happy with a chance to be a part of this open flower, an immense sea of new creation?

At Eddie's funeral Mass, on a wintry December day, a butterfly flew above the altar – much to the amazement of the congregation – towards the rafters of the church. It seemed to be a message from the other side telling us Eddie was no longer in an uncomfortable position. At the graveside we sang a song his friends composed the night before, based on the words in that last letter. Later, on our way from the graveyard, some young people, who'd been attending the burial service for their young friend killed in a motorbike accident, came over to tell us that, on hearing our singing, they were cheered up – surely a last act of love on this earth from Eddie for them. His gravestone carried an inscription from the New Testament he'd received as a personal motto from Chiara Lubich, who founded the Focolare Movement:[39] 'But God chose what is foolish in the world to shame the wise' (1 Cor 1:27).[40]

Nietzsche's famous phrase, taken up by psychiatrist Viktor Frankl in what I think is one of the most helpful books written in psychology, *Man's Search for Meaning*,[41] is that: 'He who has a *why* to live can bear almost any *how*.' So while not all readers of this book will feel able to respond to the religious dimension of Eddie's experience, I think most people would respond to someone like Eddie who was 'able not to be able' – because Eddie certainly had a 'why' to live. So the path we're following in this book is listening to the voices of people who have really suffered, following their search for meaning in their suffering.

Why should the beautiful die?

I've used this line from Stephen Foster's song, 'Ah! May the Red Rose Live Always!' (1850), since it encapsulates one of the most basic facts of all animal and human existence – that our death is inescapable. It's odd that while some atheists today find in the various kinds of suffering we've mentioned a strong argument against the existence of a good God, they don't argue with the fact of death. One of my favourite poets, Philip Larkin, in 'Aubade' spoke of it as: 'The sure extinction that we travel to / … Not to be anywhere, / And soon; nothing more terrible, nothing more true.' Perhaps Stephen Fry and Peter Singer somehow join the rest of us in accepting death as an inescapable part of the human condition (though we don't have to be as glum as Larkin was about it).

Human belief in existence beyond death, expressed in so many ways in different cultures over tens of thousands of years, provides a wider context within which the meaning of suffering in human existence has to be re-evaluated. In fact, serious reflection on human mortality is an area as well explored as any other in human culture, going back to the first-known human burials some forty thousand years ago, discovered in Lake Mungo, New South Wales, by geologist Jim Bowler in 1969 and 1974.

The refusal to accept death as the last word has been one of the most prevalent marks of humans from the very beginning. In Ireland we have the amazing Newgrange mound (3200 BC), built to capture the first rays of the sun at dawn after the longest night of the year, on 21 December, the midwinter solstice. In this place, at the centre of the world, where heaven, earth and underworld intersect, the Boyne people expressed their experience of the mysterious answer to their search for participation in everlasting order. Here they deployed all their artistic, technological and astronomic skills to elevate mid-winter sunrise into a cosmic 'yes' between sun and earth at the zero point of their mutual forsakenness.

After the longest night of the year, at sunrise on the shortest day, the direct rays of the sun burst through the arrow roof-box over the entrance, into the slightly winding passage, to the inner chamber, which for nearly twenty minutes explodes into light. Cutting through the heart of all reality, when darkness seems to have finally enveloped the world, light shines. At the time when sun and earth seem closest to the condition of death, the promise of a new year of life dawns. If death had overtaken the people's king, then, in this place at this time, a renewal of kingship is promised through attunement to the silent rebirth of the whole cosmos.[42]

A millennium later, there's Babylon's tragic *Epic of Gilgamesh* (circa 2100 BC) with Gilgamesh's pursuit of immortality, only to find out that while immortality is in his grasp (in the form of the skin-renewing, therefore immortal, serpent) it's not in his control. Around the same time there's ancient Egypt's 'Dispute of a Man Concerning Suicide with his Soul' (circa 2000 BC) in which the author seeks, through death, to reach the immortal sun god Ra in order to save his people from moral destruction. Or, among many Hindu writings, the Brihadaranyaka Upanishad's prayer (circa 700 BC):

From the unreal, lead me to the real!
From darkness lead me to light!
From death lead me to immortality! (I, iii, 28)

There are also vast libraries of Buddhist writings on the relationship between this life and what lies beyond.

The whole sequence of classic Greek philosophy represents a major breakthrough in the human exploration of the openness of the human condition to the divine, sharply summarised in Aristotle's recommendation in Book Ten, Chapter Seven of his *Nicomachean Ethics* that we should 'immortalise' as much as possible – live this life oriented to the beyond. And the Jewish and Christian Bible recounts the experience of the dialogue between the divine I AM addressing each human being as a You-for-God, culminating in God the Father's offering us divine adoption in his Son.

The classic artists in Western literature, music, painting and architecture continue the explorations of the meaning of human existence, suffering and death, in the light of their experience of what lies beyond death. In *The Brothers Karamazov*, Dostoevsky's most explicit attention to what lies beyond death can be found in Book Six, 'On the Russian Monk', and in the epilogue. As I've written elsewhere, even Samuel Beckett 'felt it was no accident he was born on Good Friday. And that bare turning around of the Forsaken One's "into Thy hands" may just about be alluded to in his famous 'I can't go on, I must go on …'[43]

We've already mentioned Viktor Frankl: here is the well-known key insight from his concentration camp experience, again pointing to a horizon beyond physical death, yet in language a non-believer might still respond to:

> A thought transfixed me: for the first time in my life I saw the truth as it is set into song by so many poets, proclaimed as the final wisdom by so many thinkers. The truth – that love is the ultimate and the highest goal to which Man can aspire. Then I grasped the meaning of the greatest secret that human poetry and human thought and belief have to impart: *The salvation of Man is through love and in love.* I understood how a man who has nothing left in this world still may know bliss, be it only for a brief moment, in the contemplation of his beloved. In a position of utter desolation, when Man cannot express himself in positive action, when his only achievement may consist in enduring his sufferings in the right way – an honourable way – in such a position Man can, through loving contemplation of the image he carries of his beloved, achieve fulfilment.[44]

Perhaps the horizon within which atheists like Stephen Fry and Peter Singer think about suffering and death could be widened a little further by more contact with the major sources of human reflection on these matters alluded to here. The voices of those we will be listening to in the next few chapters offer invitations, not arguments, but for me they carry the kind of evidence bestowed by the authority of their suffering.

FOUR: CHIARA LUCE BADANO

'If you want it, Jesus, I want it too'

As I've said earlier, as soon as I'd heard Stephen Fry's question, 'bone cancer in children – what's that about?' I thought about Chiara Luce Badano from Sassello, a little town west of Genoa in Italy. On 7 October 1990 she died of bone cancer – an illness particularly prevalent in young people. On 25 September 2010 she was declared Blessed at the sanctuary of Our Lady of Divine Love outside Rome in a ceremony attended by twenty-five thousand people. To ask why she was declared blessed is, I think, one of the ways I'd try to answer Stephen Fry's question. But, as Jacopo Lubich remarks, she gives an example of living that can work for anyone, whether Christian, agnostic or atheist, simply because she shows by her life what Love – spelt, with a capital L – means.[45]

Like all teenagers, on weekends Chiara wanted to stay out late with her friends in the local café, and hated having to come home while her friends were still there. 'One day she said: "I feel like Cinderella who, at midnight, had to run off and who lost her shoe."'[46] Her last four months of life were cheered up by the

Italian team's performance in the World Cup, where she was a fan of their brilliant forward, Salvatore Schillaci.[47] Only eight days before she died, she asked her parents to buy the next stage in the English language course she was studying.[48] And the quote I've used to head this chapter was her answer to the anguished question anyone struggling to reconcile their faith with suffering surely asks at some time or another, 'why me?' or, as Chiara Badano put it, 'Why, Jesus?'[49] While it's not possible to give a fully rounded picture of her in one short chapter, here's at least one example of her sense of humour in a note for her father:

> I, the undersigned Badano Chiara bestow at 12.45 on the 14th inst. 2 kisses on my father Badano Fausto Ruggero who promises for 30 days, under pain of 1 day of fast, not to utter further the above-mentioned phrase: give me a little kiss. Read, approved and signed, Chiara Badano.

Becoming Chiara Luce

We'll try to understand how the attitude towards suffering she developed as her illness progressed existed in embryo form from early childhood. Chiara Luce Badano was born on 29 October 1971 in Sassello, a small town in northern Italy with a population of about eighteen hundred. She was the only child of Teresa and Ruggero Badano, who'd been waiting for a child for eleven years after they'd married. Ruggero was a truck driver, and Teresa worked in a biscuit factory. From her dad (who later in life felt he'd been unduly strict with her when she was young) she was to inherit a love for the truth, a search for justice and an attentiveness to the poor. From her mother she learned gentleness, perseverance and great faith. Chiara Luce loved getting her parents to tell the story of how they'd met and fallen in love, always ribbing her mother that she'd played hard to get.

Teresa: '[We tried] to bring her up with love, which includes the truth, but never in an authoritarian way – one time after a little row, Chiara went to her room, slamming the door after her. After a while, Teresa quietly called her name. No answer. Another time. No answer. Then, "What, Mommy?" I asked her to open the door, and she did. Then, as sweetly as I could, "Now you can close the door again, but without slamming it." She looked me right in the eye, then with a big effort, she closed it the way I asked her to.'

Her youthful dreams showed a maturity well beyond her years. For instance, in her first essay at school she wrote: 'I dream of a day in which the children of slaves and their masters will sit together at the table of fraternity just like Jesus with the apostles.'

Amazingly, at just seven and a half years of age, she wrote a reflective piece showing remarkable insight:

One day you're born. No one asked you if you wanted to live. But now you're living. Sometimes it's nice for you. Sometimes instead you are sad. There are many things you don't understand. You're alive, but why are you alive? With your hands you must help to re-order the world. With your mind you must try to distinguish good and evil. With your heart you must love people and help them when you can. There are many tasks awaiting you. They await our hands, our mind, and our heart.

As a child, Chiara Luce's experiences weren't that different from other children. Once, when her mother asked her to clear the table, she said, 'No, I don't want to.' She got as far as her room, then turned back and said, 'Mom, I've just remembered that story in the Gospel about the two workers who had to go and work in the vineyard; one said "yes" but didn't go; the other instead said "no" … Mom, give me that apron.' And she started clearing up.

When she was nine she made a renewed decision to take the Gospel more seriously. She decided to learn to live the Gospel one sentence or phrase at a time, just like we learn the alphabet one letter at a time. In 1985 she wrote: 'I've discovered the Gospel in a new light. I've understood that I haven't been an authentic Christian because I haven't been living it deeply. Now I want to make this magnificent book the only goal of my life. I can't remain illiterate of such an extraordinary message. Just as it's easy for me to learn the alphabet, in the same way I must learn to live the Gospel.'[50]

This commitment arose after she and her mother had attended a summer gathering of mostly lay men, women and children who belonged to the Focolare Movement which, as I wrote earlier, is a group devoted to living out the Gospel in order to help fulfil Jesus' prayer 'that all may be one'. They were struck by its atmosphere and so decided to keep in touch. Chiara Luce now began to live the Gospel not just on her own but together with others. Throughout her teenage years she travelled to other towns to meet up with friends who had decided to share their journey to God together. And it wasn't all prayers! She had a great friend, Chicca, and together with other friends they listened to Bruce Springsteen and U2, enjoyed each other's company and went on holidays together.

In little ways she tried to foster mutual love within her family. At home she took on the role of educator, even advising her father: 'Dad, when you get up early in the morning don't draw the blinds so that mom can continue sleeping!' Or when she convinced her mother to make up with her sister-in-law after an ongoing row.

Her strong character and willpower were always and everywhere in evidence. When she was gifted money for her Confirmation she gave it away to the poor. Once, during a fund-raising event, she gave away her favourite watch because it was quite valuable. Her parents gave her another one but she gave that away too a few days later!

She loved tennis, swimming, skating, but she was also an avid reader. She read Dostoevsky's *The Idiot*, Goethe's *The Sorrows of Young Werther*, Joseph Roth's *The Legend of the Holy Drinker*, Hemingway's *The Old Man and the Sea*, and Richard Bach's *Jonathan Livingston Seagull*. And her favourite book was Antoine de Saint-Exupéry's *The Little Prince*. As she grew into her teens she wondered what she might do when she grew up: perhaps she'd be an air hostess, or a paediatrician who'd go to Africa to help children.

Her basic desire to live the Gospel was ratified; following a young people's meeting in 1983, she shared her new-found joy in a letter to Chiara Lubich. In her letter she referred to a point of the Focolare spirituality of unity that focuses on Jesus' cry on the Cross, 'My God, my God, why have you forsaken me?' as the moment when Jesus reunited us with God and with one another. For a member of the Focolare, to choose to love Jesus Forsaken means to try to meet him and to love him in the difficult circumstances and situations of life. In this light, Chiara

Luce wrote: 'I rediscovered Jesus Forsaken in a special way. I experienced him in every person that passed by me. This year I've made a new resolution to see Jesus Forsaken as my spouse and to welcome him joyfully and, above all, with all the love possible.'[51]

A note that came to light after her death underlines her desire to devote her life towards others: 'My friend has scarlet fever and everyone is too scared to visit her. With my parents' permission I decided to do my homework over at her place so she wouldn't feel lonely.' Chiara Luce loved to spend the afternoons or evenings in Bar Gino, one of the town's cafés, with her wide circle of teenage friends.[52]

The twenty-five minute decision

The summer of 1988, her seventeenth year, marked a very important turning point in her life because of two distressing events, the first of which her mother called 'her first big suffering'.[53] Chiara Luce had just learned that she'd failed maths at school and wrote to her parents from Rome, where she was accompanying a group of younger girls going to a big Focolare meeting: 'This is a very important moment for me: failing my exam is a meeting with Jesus crucified and forsaken on the cross.'

What happened the following autumn, however, was far more serious. While playing tennis, she felt a very sharp pain in her shoulder. When the pain didn't go away, she had to undergo a series of intensive tests. The verdict: osteosarcoma, one of the most aggressive and painful forms of bone cancer. At just seventeen, this was devastating news.

Her mother recalls the day the test results revealed just how serious the situation was. It was 14 June 1989 when Chiara Luce was once again admitted to the hospital in Turin for a few days. Following a conversation with the consultant, she realised how terribly serious her illness was, with little hope of recovery. Teresa recalls seeing her walking slowly and silently to the house where they were staying.

When she got home, Teresa, who had herself been ill and unable to accompany Chiara Luce on the hospital visit, wanted to speak to her, but she said, 'don't say anything, Mom'. She went and lay face down on her bed for twenty-five minutes, which her parents now believe were the most important twenty-five minutes of her life. Teresa had the wisdom not to interfere. When Chiara Luce eventually came in to her, she spoke to Teresa with a radiant smile and said, 'You can speak now, Mom!' Somehow, Chiara Luce, who, like every young person, wanted to live, had said 'Yes' to her new situation. She'd made her decision and there would be no going back. Her mother noticed a new glow in her face and words. Whatever struggle had gone on in her heart had been resolved through a deep conversation with God.[54]

The doctor broke the news that Chiara Luce's illness was incurable:

Teresa: 'I felt so terrible that I said to Ruggero: "When I die, don't write the date of my death on my tomb, but today's date, because I have died today, in this moment" … But naturally you go on. You understand that you can't stop. And Jesus gives you the strength to keep going and to repeat that "yes" each time he asks you. Also, so our sorrow wouldn't weigh Chiara down. But it was such a mutual love that at the end you could say that we each supported the other: Chiara lived for us, and we for her.'

Teresa: 'When the doctor gave me a prescription, he said, "This is the therapy – but before my therapy, you keep administering yours to Chiara." And my "therapy" was the strength of the Holy Spirit, who surrounded, guided and transformed us.'

Ruggero: 'Thinking back over the time of Chiara's illness, we could only say that they were the two years of our lives most blessed by God.'

Eventually, she was admitted to a hospital in Turin. 'At first we thought we'd visit her to keep her spirits up,' one of the boys she knew said, 'but very soon we understood that, in fact, we were the ones who needed her. Her life was like a magnet drawing us to her.' Now came the time for her to reaffirm and live her love for Jesus Forsaken in a big way. It's impressive to see how much Chiara Luce remained faithful to him throughout the whole course of her illness. In doing so, she expressed her love for God and her love for others. When Cardinal Saldarini of Turin visited her in hospital, he was struck by her face and said: 'You have a marvellous light in your eyes. How come?' After a moment's pause, she replied: 'I try to love Jesus.'[55]

Serious illness can mean the gradual erosion of our independence, while physical suffering wears down our natural capacities. Chiara Luce accepted these privations, including the loss of her hair from chemotherapy and increasingly compromised mobility. For each lock of hair that fell she'd say, 'For you, Jesus.' She felt each day God was asking small and big demands on her, including the loss of contact with many of her Focolare friends. To one she wrote:

I've gone out of your life in an instant ... Oh how I'd have loved to stop that train taking me farther and farther away! But I still didn't understand. I was still too full with so many ambitions, projects and who knows what (things that now seem so unimportant, meaningless and passing). Another world was waiting for me, and all I had to do was abandon myself to it. But now I feel enveloped in a splendid plan which is being revealed to me, little by little.[56]

Putting aside her own need to rest, she spent time walking around the wards with a drug-dependent girl who suffered from serious depression. This meant getting out of bed despite the pain caused by the huge growth on her spine. 'I'll have time to rest later,' she said. When she lost the use of her legs, Chiara Luce said, 'If I'd to choose between walking or going to heaven, I'd choose going to heaven.'

Everyone who knew her prayed for a miracle. Someone suggested that she might go to Lourdes, but she said: 'If Our Lady wants to do a miracle for me, she can do it here too. And if that's not the will of God I ask Mary for the strength to never slacken.' To her father, who was clearly greatly burdened by the situation, Chiara Luce advised, 'You've got to break it up into pieces, Dad, live each moment well in union with Jesus.'[57]

Time can't be stopped

In 1989 she was already undergoing painful medical treatment for a tumour, but wanted to keep up her studies, so a teacher tutored her in Italian literature. For her teacher, she wrote an essay on the value of time. It's like a commentary on 'vanity of vanities, all is vanity'. Jacopo Lubich sees this reflection as helping to explain how she could endure such physical and mental suffering.[58] The inscription on the wall beside the sundial she's talking about is in front of her local church at Sassello – it's the famous line in Virgil's *Georgics*: '*Fugit irreparabile tempus*' or 'time flies irretrievably':

This Latin inscription on the wall of an old building next to a sundial, reminds us, every time we raise our eyes to it, that our days, every one of them, fly by quickly. The wisdom of our fathers, recorded in these few words, causes us to pause for a moment and reflect on the meaning of our lives that so often run away in triviality, because they are suffocated by a boring daily routine, or by the frantic course which the modern way of living sometimes forces on us. If we think about it, we will realise that often a person does not live his life at all, because he is immersed in a time that does not even exist, in memories or in regrets.

In reality, the only time a person has is the present moment, which should be lived within ourselves, taking full advantage of it. If a person lives in this way, he will certainly feel free, for he will no longer be crushed by anguish over his past or his future. Certainly, being able to achieve this goal is not simple and needs a constant effort to give a meaning to each action, no matter how great or how small, for others.

Come to think of it, everyone is already working for others, even the worker hammering a bolt or the farmer planting a field, only that the real and important meaning of work is often lost. Perhaps if we gave a new intention to our actions, we would feel more fulfilled and be more conscious of the value of our life that is a precious gift not to be spoiled or burnt away in empty and useless ambitions.[59]

On her eighteenth birthday she received many gifts of money. But she said, 'it's no use to me, I have everything'. When Teresa asked what she should do with the money, Chiara Luce replied: 'Listen to the Holy Spirit, the money is his and he'll tell you.' Eventually the money was sent to a project in Chad for street children.

Conscious of her declining health, her inner resolve strengthened. In July 1990 the chemotherapy treatment ceased. In a letter of 19 July 1990, Chiara Luce wrote, 'They've stopped the chemotherapy. Medicine has laid down its arms! Now only God can do something.'[60] She once again commented to her mother that around her everyone was asking for a miracle but she felt she wasn't able to ask for it because it was becoming clear that such a miracle was not God's will.

If you want it, Jesus, I want it too

She grew ever more aware that her suffering was a gift. For instance, she was soon telling others: 'Don't ask Jesus to bring me to heaven. Otherwise he might think I don't want to suffer any more. He'll come to take me when the time is right.' To her mother, 'Mom if they asked me if I'd want to get back walking again I'd reply "no" because in this way I'm nearer to Jesus.'[61]

Despite her resolve, she still had her moments of anguish. Would she manage to be faithful to Jesus Forsaken and live her ultimate encounter with Him in death? She remarked: 'I feel so small and the road ahead so hard. Often I feel overwhelmed by suffering. But it's my spouse who's coming to visit me, right?' She found the strength to say often, 'Yes, I'll repeat …: "if you want it, Jesus, I want it too."'[62]

Struck by a spiritual message Chiara Lubich shared around that time – that Jesus' suffering and pain freely accepted were necessary to redeem the world, Chiara Luce assured her friends that 'I'll offer everything to Jesus'. In a note composed just before a large gathering of young people from Focolare, she wrote: 'I offer my nothingness so that the Holy Spirit may pour out on the young people all the gifts of his love, light and peace so that everyone may understand what an immense free gift life is and how important it is to live it in every moment in the fullness of God. In my staying [referring to Mary who stood by the Cross] is your going.'[63] She offered her sufferings for the Church. For instance, she told Chiara Lubich, who'd been invited to be a lay observer at a Synod of Bishops, that she'd offer her sufferings for the success of that event.

Throughout all of this period she was accompanied by her parents, relations and especially the many young Focolare friends she'd journeyed with for many years. And her focus was to see how she could best love them. On Valentine's Day in 1990 she herself booked a meal for her parents at a local restaurant. As they got ready to go out, Chiara Luce said to them from her bed, 'this evening look one another in the eyes, and don't come home before midnight!' and then to her mother: 'and remember, Mum, before me, there was Dad.'

She kept radiating her union with God with a surprising wisdom. The local bishop who visited her was deeply struck by her maturity, as were her many young visitors. When asked by her mother did she speak of God to her friends, she replied:

'No. There's no point in speaking of God, I have to give him.' Chiara Lubich commented when she saw a photo of Chiara Luce towards the end of her life: 'I think there's something special in her that couldn't be invented. It's not just joy she has in her eyes but something more, I would say the light of the Spirit.'[64]

On the last day of her life many young people waited outside her room. She wanted to greet them. Her mother was reluctant to let them in but Chiara Luce insisted, taking off her oxygen mask in order to greet them all. She explained to Teresa: 'Mom, young people are the future. I can no longer run. I want to hand the torch over to them like they do at the Olympics. Young people have only one life – it's worth spending it well.'

On the afternoon of 6 October 1990, Chiara Luce made a gesture for Teresa to come closer. She hugged her mother and put her hand on her hair. With a great effort she told her with all the strength she had left: 'Bye, Mom! Be happy, because I'm happy.'

Ruggero: 'From the other side of the bed I asked her if that held for me too. Then with great effort she turned to me and nodded yes with her head, with a beautiful smile. [A few hours later, Chiara Luce died.]

Maria Teresa: 'Yes, just after 4 a.m. on the morning of 7 October 1990. We embraced and then knelt down beside her bed and said the Creed together. Then we said the words of Sacred Scripture: "God has given, God has taken away, blessed be God."'

Ruggero: 'I said to Teresa: Now we will no longer see her.'

Maria Teresa: 'Those words expressed all Ruggero's sorrow along with mine. Then I replied: "No Ruggero, we've accompanied her to the gates of Paradise. The gates have opened, she's gone in, then they've closed again. We can't enter, but a tiny bit of our love has gone in with Chiara. Because love never dies.'"

'Her life: A wonderful message'

Her doctor, a non-believer and a strong critic of the Church, was deeply touched by the way Chiara and her parents had been living. 'Since I met Chiara something changed inside me. There's coherence here, and here I can understand Christianity.' Another doctor, Antonio Delogu, said, 'Through her smile, and through her eyes full of light, she showed us that death doesn't exist; only life exists.'[65] As I've mentioned, twenty-five thousand young people attended Chiara's beatification in 2010 and many said that through her they discovered that holiness was possible for them too.

Speaking to young people in Palermo, on 3 October 2010, Pope Benedict XVI remarked:

I do not want to start with a discussion but with a testimonial, a true and very timely life story. I believe you know that last Saturday, 25 September, a young Italian girl, called Chiara, Chiara Badano, was declared Blessed in Rome ... Her life was a short one but it is a wonderful message. Chiara was born in 1971 and died in 1990 from an incurable disease. Nineteen years full of life, love and faith. Her last two years were also full of pain, yet always full of love and light, a light that shone around her, that came from within: from her heart filled with God! How was this possible? How could a seventeen- or eighteen-year-old girl live her suffering in this way, humanly without hope, spreading love, serenity, peace and faith? This was obviously a grace of God, but this grace was prepared and accompanied by human collaboration as well: the collaboration of Chiara herself, of course, but also of her parents and friends.

On Sunday, 5 February 2012 Pope Benedict, reflecting on Jesus' healing the sick, recalled Chiara Luce again. He said that, 'Even in the face of death, faith can make possible what is humanly impossible. But faith in what? In the love of God. Here is the true response, the thing that radically overcomes evil. As Jesus faced evil with the power of love that comes from the Father, so we too can face and overcome the trial of sickness by keeping our hearts immersed in the love of God.' He went on to place Chiara Luce among those 'people who have borne up under terrible suffering because God gave them a deep serenity'. Blessed Chiara Badano was 'struck down in the flower of her youth by an incurable illness. How many people went to see her and received light and encouragement!'

Chiara Luce lived life to the fullest in the very moments that Stephen Fry and Peter Singer would say 'proved' it had no meaning or point, the moments they say 'we' should be raging against God for creating us in this life. Doctor Antonio Delogu's remark, 'Through her smile, and through her eyes full of light, she showed us that death doesn't exist; only life exists' embodies the luminousness of Chiara Luce's life in those final months where she is living in the Life within which our life takes place – the doctor attending her could see this in her attitude, her face. She's a living answer to the despair of the atheist feeling trapped in a worldview where this life is extinguished absolutely at death, and where this extinction drains from this life the animating sense of its transcendent significance and worth, along with its inchoate participation in an undying Life.

In our next chapter let's listen to another voice of suffering, in the story of a young woman who lived to be ten years older than Chiara Luce. Etty Hillesum's suffering came from quite different sources, yet Etty found in herself and beyond herself resources for overcoming those sufferings in a way that parallels her younger 'sister' in suffering.

FIVE: ETTY HILLESUM
'My life has become an uninterrupted dialogue with you'

As we've seen earlier, Ivan, in Dostoevsky's *The Brothers Karamazov*, returns to God his 'entrance ticket' to the world, renouncing a world created by a God who allows innocent children to suffer. In this chapter I explore the story of a young Jewish woman who chose – with astonishing courage – to stand with her people and face what she clearly saw, within an ever-deepening religious context, to be her imminent extinction in the Holocaust.

I was very moved by the earliest versions of Etty Hillesum's letters and diaries a friend in the Netherlands sent me in the early 1980s. For me they offered a particularly powerful rejoinder to the moral abyss of the National Socialist regime. The hangman's noose was gradually tightened on Dutch Jews, with the first deportations to concentration camps in the east in February 1941, while all Jews were forced to wear the Star of David badges from May 1942. Of one hundred and forty thousand Jews in the Netherlands before the war, only thirty thousand survived the Holocaust. One hundred and seven thousand were deported to the camps in the east, all but six thousand of them from Westerbork transit camp in north eastern Netherlands.

Born in the Netherlands on January 1914 to a Dutch father and Russian mother, Esther (Etty) Hillesum was one of three children. Her two siblings, Michael (Mischa), a gifted pianist, and Jacob (Jaap), a medical doctor, both suffered from mental illness. She was awarded a Master's Degree in Law at the University of Amsterdam in 1939, while also studying, and later teaching, Slavic languages. Her entire family perished in the Holocaust.

Etty's mounting dread of the approaching Holocaust

Etty's early twenties were punctuated by periods of psychological distress, but the last few years of her life were marked by an amazing spiritual transformation, triggered by her meeting the fifty-four-year-old German Jungian psychotherapist Julius Spier in February 1941. Given that the first half of her diaries are taken up with her conflicted feelings for Spier, who was divorced and engaged to a former student, it's clear that that transformation was particularly hard-won. The physical relationship Spier had with his client Etty – surely professional misconduct on his part – along with being a source of spiritual clarification for her, caused her great emotional conflict and turmoil. At the same time she continued the physical relationship she'd begun with widower Hans Wegerif, whose Amsterdam household she managed. Both men were old enough to be her father, in fact she referred to them in her diary as, 'My two grey-haired friends. What is it with me?' (20 February 1942, p. 249).[66] Spier passed away from cancer in September 1942, but all he'd taught Etty about God, suffering and acceptance flowered in a new and luminous way, as evident from the final few hundred pages of her diary and in her letters.

The inspiring figures I've referred to in this book have faced physical suffering due to illness, and, later, we'll see that Job's suffering can be understood as a deeply experienced breakdown and subsequent absence of relationship with God. Etty's suffering was mostly psychological and was surely driven and shaped in important ways by the tightening of the Nazi noose on the Jewish people in Holland, to the point that she could, with calm horror, visualize their eventual destruction, including her own:

> And now Jews may no longer visit greengrocers' shops, they will soon have to hand in their bicycles, they may no longer travel by tram, and they must be off the streets by eight o'clock at night (12 June 1942, p. 409).

> I continue to grow from day to day, even with the likelihood of destruction staring me in the face (3 July 1942, p. 463).

> For us, I think, it is no longer a question of living, but of how one is equipped for one's extinction (31 July 1943, p. 631).[67]

'Digging out God again'

The editors of her diaries and letters note how 'Felix Weinreb in his memoirs wrote: "What I found most striking was her religious sense of things, a quality that she had recently discovered in herself"' (p. 767). This flowering of her spiritual and religious openness was something that astonished those who'd known her only in the 1930s. Where Ivan Karamazov responded to the suffering and moral evil in the world by rejecting God for creating the world where such things could happen, Etty experienced an unexpected spiritual deepening in the final two years of her life. Instead of succumbing to despair she came to a profound new understanding of God and of her fellow human beings, sparked off by Spier, and developed by her meditative engagement with the Psalms, the Gospels, St Paul, St Augustine, Dostoevsky and Rainer Maria Rilke.

I was very taken by Pope Benedict XVI's words about Etty in his final public audience on Ash Wednesday, 13 February 2013. Significantly, Benedict was speaking about conversion, mentioning famous examples like St Augustine and the Russian Orthodox philosopher and theologian, Pavel Florensky. But Benedict went on to speak about Etty, quoting her diaries:

I am also thinking of Etty Hillesum, a young Dutch girl of Jewish origin who died in Auschwitz. At first far from God, she discovered him looking deep within her and she wrote: 'There is a really deep well inside me. And in it dwells God. Sometimes I am there, too. But more often stones and grit block the well, and God is buried beneath. Then he must be dug out again' (26 August 1941, p. 90). In her disrupted, restless life she found God in the very midst of the great tragedy of the twentieth century: the Shoah. This frail and dissatisfied young woman, transfigured by faith, became a woman full of love and inner peace who was able to declare: 'I live in constant intimacy with God.'

Cycling on a cold dark November morning, she prayed 'something like this,' entrusting herself completely to God and asking him: 'God, take me by Your hand, I shall follow You dutifully and not resist too much.' She asks 'now and then' to be granted 'a short respite,' but promises to 'follow wherever

Your hand leads me,' trying not to be afraid (25 November 1941, p. 154).

Why she doesn't blame God

Far from blaming God for the horrific tragedy of the impending Holocaust, Etty insists that it's human beings who are responsible for the evil-doing, not God – 'Neither do I hold You responsible. You may later hold us responsible' (12 July 1942, p. 489). Knowing only too well the motivations of those wishing to bring about her own death and that of her people, along with her growing experience of the God she addressed as 'You', she knows God can't be held responsible for evil.

Etty records a conversation with an acquaintance, Jan Boole, who'd bitterly asked, 'What is it in human beings that makes them want to destroy others?' She replied, ironically noting she's preaching at him: 'Human beings, you say, but remember that you're one yourself … The rottenness of others is in us, too … I really see no other solution than to turn inward and to root out all the rottenness there. I no longer believe that we can change anything in the world until we have first changed ourselves' (19 February 1942, p. 245). I've already quoted Solzhenitsyn's crucial insight into the mystery of human responsibility for moral evil, that 'the line dividing good and evil cuts through the heart of every human being'.[68] Etty's words are another expression of the same view, born of spiritual growth in the face of terrible injustice and suffering.

Wil van den Bercken has noted two other comments of Etty that express her intense awareness of the human responsibility for the evil she's confronting:

All disasters stem from us. Why is there a war? Perhaps because now and then I might be inclined to snap at my neighbour. Because I and my neighbour and everyone else do not have enough love. Yes we could fight war and all its excrescences by releasing, each day, the love that is shackled inside us and giving it a chance to live (27 March 1942, p. 307).

And again he points out that 'in her writings, she repeatedly expresses the thought that man is the cause of evil: "no matter what monstrous dimensions it may sometimes assume ... it originates in man, in each individual, in myself, which makes everything understandable and ensures that deeds never become isolated monsters, which have nothing to do with human beings"' (27 March 1942, p. 307).[69]

Etty's task of 'helping God'

Not only does she exonerate God of responsibility for the suffering of the Jewish people, but speaks of helping him, since it seems as if he's unable to change what's happening:

if God does not help me to go on, then I shall have to help God ... I don't fool myself about the real state of affairs, and I've even dropped the pretense that I'm out to help others. I shall merely try to help God as best I can, and if I succeed in doing that, then I shall be of use to others as well (11 July 1942, pp. 484–5).

This is one of her fullest statements on her extraordinary transfiguration of the meaning of her suffering at the hands of her fellow men into an act of seeking to bring God's love to everyone, friend and foe alike, in this hell on earth.

We are reminded of the representative consciousness of a prophet like Jeremiah, speaking and *being* on behalf of a whole people:

> I shall try to help You, God, to stop You ebbing away in me, though I cannot vouch for it in advance. But one thing is becoming increasingly clear to me: that You cannot help us, that we must help You to help ourselves. And that is all we can manage these days and also all that really matters: that we safeguard that little piece of You, God, in ourselves. And perhaps in others as well. Alas, there doesn't seem to be much You Yourself can do about our circumstances, about our lives (12 July 1942, pp. 488–9; van den Bercken's revised translation, *Proceedings*, 162).

What does 'helping God' mean in what she called her 'Sunday morning prayer' of 12 July 1942? Van den Bercken notes that here 'she comes to the same conclusion as her contemporary, Dietrich Bonhoeffer',[70] and notes that 'the development of the image of a powerless God, or rather a God renouncing his power, is also the great significance of Ivan Karamazov's *Legend of the Grand Inquisitor*'.[71] In a later chapter I'll discuss the experience of Jesus in his forsakenness on the cross, where, in the Christian understanding, Jesus, Man and God, allows himself to be crucified for all humankind. As a Jew, Etty could draw on Moses' offering himself in the place of his people, and Isaiah's prophecy of the Suffering Servant who will save his people from their sins, nor does she seem to be far from what St Paul referred to: 'in my flesh I complete what is lacking in Christ's afflictions for the sake of his body, that is, the Church' (Col 1:24).

Saint Augustine spoke of God being able to bring good out of evil (*Enchiridion*, Ch. 3 §11), and Etty's words and actions (staying on and refusing escape in order to share her people's fate) show her complete conviction that 'helping God' is precisely her way to live the awful circumstances she and her Jewish people were forced to accept. A few days later she fully endorses her friend Liesl's remark, 'It is a great privilege, isn't it, that we have been chosen to bear all this?' (14 July 1942, p. 542), and further on quotes Matthew 26:39: 'Not *my* will, but Thy will be done' (3 October 1942, p. 542). Leaving a fully worked-out theodicy to theologians, Etty is freely and intuitively living out Augustine's maxim as she herself seems to accept all that's happening as God's will for her. She's certain all that's best in her will survive: 'If all this suffering does not help us to broaden our horizon, to attain a greater humanity by shedding all trifling and irrelevant issues, then it will all have been for nothing' (24 July 1942, p. 502). Another prayer seems to heighten her acceptance of the suffering God has permitted her to undergo: 'Oh God, to bear the suffering you have imposed on me and not just the suffering I have chosen for myself' (2 October 1942, p. 538).

When one of her acquaintances, Werner, said they must develop 'a hard shell', she noted in her diary: 'A "hard shell" won't fit me; I shall remain defenceless and open to everything.' And she made this prayer: 'Dear God, what will happen to me? No, I shall not ask You beforehand, I shall bear every moment, even the most unimaginable, as it comes, and if You should ever stumble over me I shall pick You up again. I hope with You to come through' (14 or 15 July 1942, p. 495). Astonishingly, she's saying that if He trips up over her, that's because of her and she'll help Him to His feet!

I think this acceptance of God's place in her life explains what she means by 'forgiving God': 'This slice of the epoch in which we live is something I can bear, that I can shoulder without collapsing under its heavy weight, and I can already forgive God for allowing things to be as they probably must be. To have enough love in oneself to be able to forgive God!!' (Letter to Julius Spier, circa July 1942, p. 565). Where did she get this incredible surplus of love? Surely it is the result of her continual life of dialogue with God. We've already quoted Pope Benedict recalling the evocative words where Etty speaks of her soul as a well, filled with the divine Presence, even if sometimes clogged with fallen debris needing to be cleared away.

Here is one of her most luminous expressions of the core of her existence as a human being addressed as 'you' by the divine 'You', where Westerbork concentration camp fades into nothing on her living altar of thanksgiving:

My life has become an uninterrupted dialogue with You, O God, one great dialogue. Sometimes when I stand in some corner of the camp, my feet planted on Your earth, my eyes raised toward Your heaven, tears sometimes run down my face, tears of deep emotion and gratitude. At night, too, when I lie in my bed and rest in You, O God, tears of gratitude run down my face, and that is my prayer. (18 August 1943, p. 640)[72]

While the first published account of Etty's life and diaries was called An Interrupted Life,[73] rather than 'interrupt' her life, National Socialism actually intensified what she calls her 'uninterrupted dialogue' with God.

Etty's refusal to escape

Nowhere is Etty's steadfast determination to shoulder suffering as part of God's plan for her more evident than in her refusal to accept the many opportunities friends offered her to escape into hiding – a determination stemming always, it seems, from her awareness that she exists not just for herself, but for her people. This experience of representing humanity, including representatively suffering for humanity, shines through in almost everything she writes. While she did all she could to help her family accompany her gifted pianist brother, Mischa, to Barneveld, a special camp for privileged members of the Dutch Jewish community, she emphasized, 'remember: not me!' (21 June 1943, p. 604). Rather than being 'exempted',[74] she saw her very identity as bound up with the common suffering of her people. If it comes to it that she must die, how she faces that last moment will express who she is – though I'd add that the life she lived in those last few years defined who she really was, and not just that last moment in November 1943 in Auschwitz:

> I certainly do not want to go out of some sort of masochism, to be torn away from what has been the basis of my existence these last few years. But I don't think I would feel happy if I were exempted from what so many others have to suffer. They keep telling me that someone like me has a duty to go into hiding because I have so many things to do in life, so much to give. But I know that whatever I may have to give to others, I can give it no matter where I am, here in the circle of my friends or over there, in a concentration camp. And it is sheer arrogance to think oneself too good to share the fate of the masses. And if God Himself

should feel that I still have a great deal to do, well then, I shall do it after I have suffered what all the others have to suffer. And whether or not I am a valuable human being will become clear only from my behaviour in more arduous circumstances. And if I should not survive, how I die will show me who I really am (11 July 1942, p. 487).[75]

Her decision is to share in that common Jewish destiny since it will bring her in contact with the whole of humanity, including her 'so-called enemies' (24 September 1942, p. 530): 'that part of our common destiny that I must shoulder myself; I strap it tightly and firmly to my back, it becomes part of me as I walk through the streets even now' (19 July 1942, p. 484). So she can write:

And now it seems that I have been 'exempted'. 'Am I expected to jump for joy?' I asked the notary with the short leg. I don't want that scrap of paper for which most Jews would give their right arm, I don't want it in the least, so why should it have dropped into mine of all laps? I want to be sent to every one of the camps that lie scattered all over Europe, I want to be at every front, I don't ever want to be what they call 'safe', I want to be there, I want to fraternize with all my so-called enemies, I want to understand what is happening and share my knowledge with as many as I can possibly reach ... (2 October 1942, p. 541).

'I believe in God and I believe in man'

While her relationship with God is a key element for understanding how Etty dealt with suffering, it also included her relationship with her fellow men and women. As she put it herself,

'I believe in God and I believe in man' (20 June 1942, p. 434), and it's in relationship with every human being as human that she spells out just how she transforms suffering into something quite different. Somehow or other, she has a laser-like ability to get to the personal heart of each situation. Her description of her attendance at a Nazi registration office for Jews typifies this gift:

> When it was my turn to stand in front of his desk, he bawled at me, 'What the hell's so funny?' I wanted to say, 'Nothing's funny here except you', but refrained. 'You're still smirking,' he bawled again. And I, in all innocence, 'I didn't mean to, it's my usual expression.' And he, 'Don't give me that, get the hell out of here,' his face saying, 'I'll deal with you later.' And that was presumably meant to scare me to death, but the device was too transparent. I am not easily frightened. Not because I am brave, but because ... I know that these young men are merely [word missing – 'harmless'?] as long as they cannot do harm but that they become morally dangerous when they are turned loose on humanity. Yet only the system that uses such people is criminal, not these fellows. What needs eradicating is the evil in man, not man himself. (27 February 1942, pp. 258–9)[76]

Overcoming humiliation

Like Socrates, who told his accusers, 'I owe a greater obedience to God than to you' (*Apology*, 29d), Etty was convinced her spiritual self couldn't be captured or destroyed. Her inner equilibrium, maintained with courage, was more than a match for an arrogant Nazi bully:

Humiliation always involves two. The one who does the humiliating, and the one who allows himself to be humiliated. If the second is missing, that is, if the passive party is immune to humiliation, then the humiliation vanishes into thin air. All that remains are vexatious measures that interfere with daily life but are not humiliations that weigh heavily on the soul …We may of course be sad and depressed by what has been done to us; that is only human and understandable. However, our greatest injury is one we inflict upon ourselves … True peace will come only when every individual finds peace within himself; when we have all vanquished and transformed our hatred for our fellow human beings of whatever race – even into love one day, although perhaps that is asking too much. It is, however, the only solution … It means gathering together all the strength one can, living one's life with God and in God and having God dwell within (20 June 1942, pp. 434–5, 439).

Overcoming hatred by not reciprocating it

So Etty has a two-pronged strategy in overcoming suffering – first in not allowing herself to hate, and second in situating herself within the far richer and more complex horizon of divine providence, rather than the narrow 'harmony' Ivan Karamazov rejected as unacceptable because of the suffering of innocent children. She recalls a conversation with her communist friend, Klaas Smelik (senior): 'It is the only thing we can do, Klaas, I see no alternative: each of us must turn inward and destroy in himself all that he thinks he ought to destroy in others. And remember that every atom of hate we add to this world makes it still more inhospitable.' And when Klaas, 'dogged old class fighter' he's always been, objects, 'But that – that is nothing but Christianity!' she replies, 'Yes, Christianity, and why ever not?' (23 September 1942, p. 529).

While it's not possible here to do justice to the many facets of Etty's personality and life, it would be quite wrong to give the impression that she was impassive in the face of suffering. The hundreds of pages of her diary in which she struggles for emotional balance in her relationship with Spier, and the occasional references to how deeply seared by suffering she was at Westerbork, show how racked she was by its real and profound evils. An anecdote from Friedrich Weinreb's memoir lets us see her reaction to the arrival of prisoners at Westerbork from Vught, a far crueller camp:

She couldn't speak a word, only cry. She sat on a chair between Weyl's bed and mine, with her face buried in a handkerchief. Loonstijn called out: 'My good girl, for heaven's sake stop, we have troubles enough, we don't need any wailing women around'. This helped a bit, and Etty started telling us what she'd seen … But Etty said, presumably to make amends for her tearful beginning, that some of the prisoners were also smiling, and were feeling hopeful now that they had left from Vught. However, Etty soon started crying again. We let her do so, and it did help – at least then you don't have to cry yourself.[77]

Positively, the love she experienced from Spier, and where that love led her, grounds her to the point that she can tell her friend Henney, soon after Spier's death:

My most precious and most radical experience, has become so much a part of my heaven, even in my lifetime, arching above me, that no matter where in the world I am, I have only to lift up my eyes to have him with me. And even if I were locked away in an underground cell, that heaven would stretch out within me ... I am inwardly very calm, and strange though it may sound, very happy. Happy, because God has given me the strength to bear everything and to face up to it, and because with me, just as with you, gratitude will always be greater than sorrow (11 September 1942, p. 567). Her gratitude, she explains in a letter to another friend is 'gratitude that he was part of my life' (15 September 1942, p. 567).

In the midst of everything, an astonishing harmony ...

Etty prays to God: 'I promise You to strive my whole life long for beauty and harmony and also meekness and real love ...' (12 December 1941, p. 175; translation revised by Wil van den Bercken).[78] And we can see that it's not only her harmony within herself or with others that gave a richer context to her suffering. Etty also experienced deep harmony with nature – as if, despite the surrounding horror, nevertheless nature's own harmony testified to the reassuring deeper harmony of all existence. (Reminding us of the great 'nevertheless' of Psalm 73 [72]:23-28, where the divine Presence holds our hand, and accompanies us through the horror of the present age.) She has a long entry on the jasmine she can see from her window in Amsterdam:

Oh, yes, the jasmine. My God, how is it possible, it stands there squeezed between the neighbours' bare wall and the garage, overlooking the flat, dark, muddy garage roof. It is so radiant, so virginal, so unrestrained and so tender among all that greyness and that muddy darkness, an exuberant young bride lost in a back street. I can't take in how beautiful this jasmine is. But there is no need to. It is enough simply to believe in miracles in the twentieth century. And I do, even though the lice will be eating me up in Poland before long. That jasmine, words fail me when it comes to that jasmine. (1 July 1942, p. 459)

Having been moved by the sight of the jasmine, along with the climbing red roses and 'a host of pansies on a low garden wall' on her way to see Spier, she asked him, 'Isn't it almost godless to keep having such faith in God in times like these? And isn't it frivolous … to go on finding life so beautiful?' (2 July 1942, p. 459). It's in this light that Etty develops some of her greatest insights into what she calls 'the art of suffering' and how to bear it:

Suffering is not beneath human dignity. I mean: it is possible to suffer with dignity and without. I mean: most of us in the West don't understand the art of suffering and experience a thousand fears instead. We cease to be alive, being full of fear, bitterness, hatred, and despair. God knows, it's only too easy to understand why. But when we are deprived of our lives, are we really deprived of very much? And I wonder if there is much of a difference between being consumed here by a thousand fears or in Poland by a thousand lice and by hunger? We have to accept death as part of life, even the most horrible of deaths. (2 July 1942, p. 459)

She ranges beyond time and space, fully aware both of present and future horrors, which are yet unable to wipe out her stronger awareness of an underlying harmony represented by the beauty of that jasmine and by God:

> And don't we live an entire life each one of our days, and does it really matter if we live a few days more or less? I am in Poland every day, on the battlefields, if that's what one can call them. I often see visions of poisonous green smoke; I am with the hungry, with the ill-treated and the dying, every day, but I am also with the jasmine and with that piece of sky beyond my window; there is room for everything in a single life. For belief in God and for a miserable end. (2 July 1942, p. 460)

Inwardly free when outwardly constrained

Etty's awareness of the inviolability of her inner self means – like the Socrates of Plato's *Apology* and *Phaedo* – that she remains inwardly free but with a richer experience of her existence as a continual You-wards dialogue with God, no matter how outwardly constrained she may be:

> Many accuse me of indifference and passivity when I refuse to go into hiding; they say that I have given up. They say everyone who can must try to stay out of their clutches, it's our bounden duty to try. But that argument is specious. For while everyone tries to save himself, vast numbers are nevertheless disappearing. And the funny thing is, I don't feel I'm in their clutches anyway, whether I stay or am sent away. I find all that talk so cliché-ridden and naive, and can't go along with it anymore. I don't feel

in anybody's clutches ... no matter whether I am sitting at this beloved old desk now, or in a bare room in the Jewish district, or perhaps in a labour camp under SS guards in a month's time – I shall always feel safe in God's arms ... And my acceptance is not indifference or helplessness. I feel deep moral indignation at a regime that treats human beings in such a way. But events have become too overwhelming and too demonic to be stemmed with personal resentment and bitterness ... I am only bowing to the inevitable, and even as I do so I am sustained by the certain knowledge that ultimately they cannot rob us of anything that matters. (11 July 1942, p. 487)

In one of her last letters from the camp, to Johanna, Klaas Smelik and others, her inner freedom seems to overcome all fears, all suffering, with a certainty she wishes to share with her friends:

All I wanted to say is this: The misery here is quite terrible; and yet, late at night when the day has slunk away into the depths behind me, I often walk with a spring in my step along the barbed wire. And then, time and again, it soars straight from my heart – I can't help it, that's just the way it is, like some elementary force – the feeling that life is glorious and magnificent, and that one day we shall be building a whole new world. Against every new outrage and every fresh horror, we shall put up one more piece of love and goodness, drawing strength from within ourselves. We may suffer, but we must not succumb. And if we should survive unhurt in body and soul, but above all in soul, without bitterness and without hatred, then we shall have a right to a say after the war. (3 July 1943, p. 613)

The art of suffering – to bear Your mysteries

Perhaps that one phrase could sum up Etty's 'art of suffering': 'we may suffer, but we must not succumb.' No matter what happened to her, Etty remained Etty, just as she had affirmed: 'I know for certain that there will be a continuity between the life I have led and the life about to begin' (28 July 1942, pp. 511–12). With a keenness always occasioned by suffering, whether at the deathbed of her beloved Spier or by the horrors all around her, that inner continuity was surely due to her having touched in the transcendence of the beloved other, whether friend or foe, the transcendence of God, for which she had her own word: mystery – the mystery of 'You' and the mystery of each 'you':

> I stood beside his bed and found myself standing before one of Your last mysteries, my God … You have placed me before Your ultimate mystery, oh God. I am grateful to You for that, I even have the strength to accept it and to know there is no answer. That we must be able to bear Your mysteries. (1 September 1942, pp. 514–15)

SIX: JOB
'Why do you hide your face and count me as your enemy?'

Rabbi Harold Kushner wrote *When Bad Things Happen to Good People* after his fourteen-year-old son died of the incurable genetic disease, progeria. One chapter of his book focused on the Book of Job in the Old Testament, as a most probing exploration of the meaning of suffering in human life, with the search for an answer to the question of God's responsibility for how such terrible things can befall innocent people.[79]

In Genesis, Adam and Eve share with their tempter the responsibility and guilt for their misfortune, but Job is shown to be a completely innocent human being. Les Murray, one of Australia's most celebrated contemporary poets, poses Job's question thus: 'Why does God not spare the innocent?' And his poem continues: 'The answer to that is not in/ the same world as the question …'[80] For Job – as it was for Chiara Luce Badano and Etty Hillesum – the question of innocent suffering can't be separated from questioning God.

Job is presented to us as the wealthiest man in the East. More important than his wealth and a large family (seen here as another possession) are his inner qualities, especially his relationship with God, which is so important to Job that he even offers sacrifice to God in case any of his children may have sinned. After we've been introduced to Job, we are made privy to a dialogue between God and Satan about Job that's definitely 'not in the same world'.

Unconditional love versus utilitarian calculation

God's pride in Job and his confidence in Job's unconditional love for him provokes Satan (whose name means 'accuser'). Satan challenges God's confidence in Job, suggesting the only reason Job 'loves' God is because of what he gets out of Him.

Because He deeply trusts Job's love for Him, God allows Satan to orchestrate a series of natural and human disasters that wipe out all his possessions and children.[81] But Job justifies God's faith in him by fully accepting his condition as a creature of God: 'naked I came from my mother's womb and naked I will depart' (1:21). So God wins the first round of the contest with Satan since Job's faith remains solid despite losing almost everything he has. Satan raises the stakes by saying it's only when Job experiences suffering in his own body that his devotion will be really tested: 'A man will give all he has for his own life. But stretch out your hand and strike his flesh and bones, and he will surely curse you to your face' (2:5).

God allows Satan to cause Job's health to deteriorate until he's on the brink of death. It seems at last Job's spirit is broken, since he sits down in the dust and despondently scrapes at his sores. When his wife urges him to die, he gives out to her, saying if we accept good things from God, we have to accept troubles too. He calls her a fool, in the sense of someone who doesn't know God. Job accepts that, as well as good, evil, 'ra' – meaning physical disasters and calamities, not moral evil – comes from God. So, with tremendous inner restraint he accepts his immense physical suffering: 'Shall we accept good from God, and not trouble [ra]?' (2:10). He has, until now, accepted that God acts only for his good – even in his permitting a litany of catastrophes – from which he's convinced good will ultimately come.

What's the author of Job trying to show us in the story so far? Well, maybe we've had relationships with people we thought were our friends, only to find that when the chips were down, they were really only using us for their own ends. He's showing us that Job's relationship with God isn't based on God supplying an unbroken stream of good experiences to him, but that Job really loves God for who God is. He's also showing us that God is not merely playing a particularly cruel game of cat and mouse with Job, but rather has unbreakable confidence that even when Job *is* physically reduced to almost zero, he'll still love Him for His own sake and not for what he can get out of that relationship. In this way the author is leading us to identify with Job no matter how grievous a loss we've suffered.

Inner suffering worse than outer

Then three friends who have come to comfort Job arrive. At first they weep with him, throw dust on themselves and then, for seven days, sit silently with him. But when they start speaking, instead of comforting him, each one in different ways insists that Job's misfortunes are proof positive that he has committed some appalling sin in the eyes of God and is being duly punished for it.

What they're saying, in essence, is that his relationship with God is broken and inauthentic, but Job disputes this interpretation.

So the author of the Book of Job tells this terrible story in a bid to clarify what exactly suffering means in the light of how we relate to God.

Now we find out that his deepest suffering isn't loss of wealth, family and health, but what he experiences as the loss of his relationship with God. And because his 'friends' focus precisely on this point, they take the place of Satan in the drama, since, like Satan, they adopt the same utilitarian approach to relationships. Again and again they'll insist he must have done something terribly wrong to deserve such a punishment. As his greatest tormentors, they continue Satan's sifting of Job's soul.

Job rejects God's world of undeserved pain

Until now, Job has accepted everything that has happened, but at the start of Chapter Three he curses the day he was born. In the chapter's opening verses he vehemently wishes for the reversal of the order of creation in Genesis. In place of Genesis' 'Let there be light,' he cries 'Let it be darkness (3)', and follows with five other curses summoning up darkness against the day he was born. Then he turns to the night of his birth, wishing for night to be wiped out by '*opel*' – a more sinister force than darkness itself, an evil gloom. He invokes Leviathan, a cosmic force of chaos and sterility, to destroy the created order (8), prays for 'dark stars' (9) because night didn't block his mother's womb to prevent his birth, 'and so hide misery from my eyes' (10).

This last plea reveals the underlying motivation for Job's rejection of creation, a kind of anti-Genesis, which culminates in his great lament, a cry of rage and sorrow unequalled in passionate intensity until Ivan's outburst in *The Brothers Karamazov* (Book Five, Chapter Four, 'Rebellion'). Unlike Ivan, for whom as an atheist, there's no one to rebel against – both the author of Job and Dostoevsky are believers, lending these outbursts greater poignancy.

Job's lament takes the form of a series of 'Whys?' The first two refer to Job's own condition (11-15; 16-19), where he cries out he'd prefer Sheol, a horrifying half-life in death under the ground, to the wretched life he's now experiencing. Terrifying as Sheol is, compared to his horror that God is treating him so badly, that place of death is an appealing underworld realm where all human beings are equal, prisoners set free, the weary given rest, and 'slaves free from their master'. The second two 'Whys?' broaden the question to include the suffering of all humanity. The fourth 'Why?' in particular, ponders the reasons why suffering afflicts everyone in the world, yet its meaning and purpose are hidden from us. Job questions why God gives existence 'to the man whose way (*derek*) is hid, hedged around by God?' (23). As Norman Habel in his great commentary on the Book of Job writes:

> This final 'why' makes the basis of Job's complaint explicitly existential. It is not the suffering or bitterness of life as such that consumes him, but the misery of meaninglessness. The futility of existence has two clear features: (a) the *derek* of life is hidden, and (b) the one who hides it is God.[82]

In biblical wisdom literature, '*derek*,' symbolizes a cluster of meanings: your personal destiny, the conduct of your life, your personal attunement to the underlying principle of divine order. For Job, all of these ways seem to have been obscured by the very One who created them and is supposed to be the origin and goal of ordered existence. At the beginning of his lament, then, Job has universalized his own condition to a 'tragic sense of life' for all humanity, a tragedy all the more anguished because it seems to have been allowed by the personal Creator-God.

The so-called friends' theology of success

As I've explained earlier, Job's 'friends' believe his loss of his children, property, wealth, social status and even health must be punishment by God for wrongdoing on his part. This is a knot in their religious belief that needs to be untied because it slowly enters into and poisons their understanding of God, what he's like, and how he wants to deal with us. They've unmoored their reasoning from God's revelation to us of who he is in his innermost Being. As Pope Francis recalls (13 January 2016):

> This is his name, through which he unveils, so to speak, his face and his heart to us. As the Book of Exodus recounts, on revealing himself to Moses he defined himself in this way: 'the Lord, a God merciful and gracious, slow to anger, and abounding in steadfast love and faithfulness'. (34:6)

The Old Testament use of the phrase 'the Lord' is a reverent way of recalling the actual personal name God revealed to Moses, 'I AM' (Ex 3:14), so we can read this passage as, 'I am a God merciful and gracious, slow to anger, and abounding in steadfast love and faithfulness.'

For those of us in the Judaeo-Christian tradition, then, there's a principle of reasoning here: if our thinking about complicated and emotional issues leads us to conclude that God is, in the words of Stephen Fry and Peter Singer, an evil, capricious, mean-minded, stupid bungler,[83] this should be a warning signal to us that, like Job's 'friends', we've lost touch with what should be our basic experience of God as He really is, full of mercy and compassion. Throughout the Book of Job, its author highlights how the utilitarian understanding of religion as a relationship where we live 'well' with a view to personal reward is wholly ill-conceived.

They're completely out of touch with the new awareness of individual response to the personal love of God deeply committed to his people, which was experienced by Isaiah, Jeremiah and Ezekiel. It's as if the friends had never heard of Abraham's personal experience of and response to God, nor of Moses' clear awareness of being addressed as a 'thou' by the divine I AM. The friends, rather, represent a derailment into a utilitarian instrumentalization of religion of the type Jesus opposed in the Pharisees and Sadducees.

Job's inner growth and deepening confidence in God

Job's personal conviction of his own innocence gives him the courage to oppose the accusations of the friends based on their pseudo-theology of success. That inner growth leads to his achieving the depth of prophetic individuality we associate with a Jeremiah, a depth of consciousness that eventually makes him realize he can stand for the whole of humanity as its representative before God.

Job's inner growth is accompanied by his deepening experience of God. Despite his frequent experiences of darkest despair – experiences aggravated by his pseudo-friends – there's a note of increasing trust in God with ever-growing resonance. Almost as if the more stridently the friends put forward their unforgiving and vindictive God, the more certain Job becomes that the God he experiences is utterly different from theirs.

Job's appeal for a law case with God

The most surprising way Job's certainty of his relationship with God is real and good is manifested in his cry to present the case for his innocence before God in a court of law.

In doing this, Job presupposes that there is common ground where he and God can meet. This has grounds in the biblical notion of law as intrinsically interpersonal – each of the Ten Commandments in Exodus is addressed to a 'thou', where the 'I' addressing each 'thou' is, as we've seen, the God revealed in Exodus as I AM WHO AM.[84]

So, at what seems a zero point for Job in Chapter Ten, his laments turn into prayer (2-7). With beautifully poetic language, he evokes the incredible intimacy of God's involvement with the creation of himself, and of every human being (8-12). Again and again he addresses God as 'You' – 'You clothed me with skin and flesh and knitted me with bones and sinews. In your love You granted me life, and your providence watched over my spirit' (11-12).

Two and a half millennia later, we found a similar You-relatedness to God in Etty Hillesum, again wrung from her out of the depths – the big spiritual outbursts, whether with Chiara

Luce, Etty or Job all seem to happen at the outer limits of human endurance and apparent failure.

All the greater then is Job's bewilderment that an apparently loving Creator should act with such apparent vindictiveness (13-17). So he concludes, 'Why did You bring me from the womb?' (18) and asks for a few days respite before he dies. But he doesn't speak any more of the region of death as somewhere to look forward to. It's rather 'a land whose light is sinister gloom!' (21). That gloom still seems to carry a glimmer of hope in a God he'd once felt so close to. As Hadjadj's Job remarks, 'How could evil make us so unhappy if we hadn't first heard of the promise of good?'[85] (Which seems parallel to Peter Singer's implicit concession that there may be a standard of goodness.)

Job cries to God to show him His face

Chapter Thirteen shows Job's growing confidence in God. Bearing false witness was a serious crime in the law of Israel. Now Job is so sure of God's fairness that he can accuse his friends before God for saying his relationship with God is compromised by hidden wrongdoing that has brought untold troubles upon him. This slander is an injustice God should correct (6-12). For the first time he has the courage to ask to see God's face: 'Yes, though he slay me, I will not wait. I will now argue my case to his face …no godless person would dare come before his face … Why do You hide your face and count me as your enemy?' (13, 14, 24).

'Why do You hide your face from me?' is a rejoinder to Stephen Fry's and Peter Singer's alienated articulation-from-without of what our relationship with God-if-He-existed would have to be. Here, at the very moment of making the breakthrough, we have

Job's cry for relationship, not for rejection. Emmanuel Levinas reflects that, 'the face is meaning in itself. Thou, thou art ... It is what cannot become a content graspable by thought; it is the uncontainable, it leads you beyond ...' Levinas was a Lithuanian-born Jewish philosopher who lost close family during the Holocaust and was in a camp for captured Jewish soldiers from 1940–5. These experiences, like Etty Hillesum's, heightened his awareness of what is essential in human encounter.[86]

It is this very 'asymmetry of the interpersonal'[87] that Job seeks in his desired-for face-to-face meeting with God, each profoundly respecting the otherness of the Other. For, unlike his friends, Job is convinced of the utter You-ness of the divine, and that he too is a you-for-God, not the abstract scarecrow the friends' shallow generalizations would show him to be.

Job's hope of a redeemer

As early as Chapter Sixteen, and again in Chapter Nineteen, Job expresses his sense of complete alienation from his friends, from God, and also from his family: 'His anger flares up against me; He counts me as his enemy ... He has alienated my kin from me ... All my bosom friends detest me and my loved ones have turned against me' (11, 13, 19). Along with the shattering of his entire social structure is the physical destruction of his own body: 'My bones stick to my skin and flesh; I escape with the skin of my teeth' (20).

Still, he's now sure he can stand face to face with another, even with this Other, in his court case against God. 'If only my case were recorded! If only it were inscribed on stone with iron stylus and lead, carved on rock forever!' (23-24). In the dark night of his trial, utterly alone, he still knows that the last word in that trial won't be the unjust sentence of condemnation uttered so often by his 'friends' (and before them, as we know, by his demonic Accuser). His affirmation, 'I *know* that my redeemer lives' (25) is the turning point of the whole book. In ancient Near Eastern sources, the affirmation, 'I know' can indicate a revelation conceded by God. Who is this redeemer ('*goel*') whose existence he is convinced of? Earlier (9:33; 16:19) he had spoken of a heavenly witness ('*ed*'), and of an arbiter ('*mokiah*'). So Habel regards the 'redeemer' here as a defence attorney who will take on the accuser-prosecutor we know isn't only the public opinion represented by the 'friends' but by Satan himself.[88]

But behind his faith in such a legal defender is his utter trust that he will be granted an open and fair relationship with God. This trust is so great it implies that God wouldn't be God, if He didn't ultimately recognize the innocence of his friend. Job is convinced that he can be a 'you' for the divine You, where that new clarity and depth of relation has been achieved by him precisely through his being stripped of anything except his bare selfhood to depend on, and his hope against hope in God's integrity. Nor does his faith and hope remove his fragility, brought down to skin, bone, heart and dust. We glimpse here the core of that deeply excavated personhood, where Job is capable of loving an Other purely for the Other's own sake, not for himself.

Deeper then than his physical and psychological nothingness is Job's spiritual being and his firm belief that he'll see God face to face. Earlier he had asked that God would remember him after death. Now, going beyond an earlier, less articulate hopefulness in the Bible, there emerges Job's clear anticipation of continuous participation in God's life: 'And after my skin has been destroyed, yet in my flesh shall I see God, whom I shall see for myself' (26, 27).

The final 'friend' Elihu's indictment of Job

The significance of Elihu's appearance in the drama is that he comes after Job's anguished appeal for a defender. But instead of taking up his case, Elihu only reinforces what the three 'friends' have said, inflicting a final savage suffering on Job. Pedantically, he spells out the educational function of suffering, offering to act as Job's defence lawyer – but only on the condition that Job admits he's in the wrong.

Elihu is suffering from an alienation from within the Jewish experience. He has been brought up within a culture centred upon the Transcendent God; but within this community there has been a sub-cultural dislocation or fall into spiritual blindness to the self-disclosure of the Face and Heart of the I AM revealed in Exodus. So his final words in Chapter Thirty Seven make explicit the God-forsakenness that haunted the other friends' case against Job too: 'God – we cannot reach him! Great in his might and justice ... He does not answer! Therefore men fear him. But even the wise of heart cannot see him' (23-24).

God enters openly into conversation with Job

Since for Elihu, even the wise can't see God, Job's quest for a relationship with God seems ridiculous and impossible. So, while the Elihu chapters unbearably increase Job's suffering, they also lead to the book's sharpest contrast.

Throughout, Job has sought two things: (i) at the level of relationship, a meeting with God, and (ii) intellectually, a meaning for his sufferings. Job has his desire for relationship with God vindicated in God's openly entering into the conversation Job has been directing towards him throughout the book. As we've said, Job's greatest suffering was his experience of alienation from God, an experience the 'friends', as if standing in for Satan, greatly aggravated. As G. K. Chesterton puts it:

> All the human beings through the story, and Job especially, have been asking questions of God. A more trivial poet would have made God enter in some sense or other in order to answer the questions ... [But] in this drama of scepticism God Himself takes up the role of sceptic ... He does ... what Socrates did. He turns rationalism against itself ... The poet has made God ironically accept a kind of controversial equality with His accusers ... He asks for the right which every prosecuted person possesses; He asks to be allowed to cross-examine the witness for the prosecution ... He asks Job who he is.[89]

God's first questioning of Job

In Chapter Three, Job had appeared to reject creation. Before God questions Job regarding his relation to creation, he first questions Job's own standing when addressing him out of the whirlwind: 'Who is this that darkens counsel by words without knowledge?' (38:2).

In the Old Testament, 'counsel' refers to the plan of God that lies behind all history. So God is saying to Job that he has failed to see His hand lying behind everything that was happened to him. Job's desire for non-existence in Chapter Three had in effect rejected God's order in the world. There, Job had argued from the meaninglessness of his own miserable condition to that of all humans, and finally to that of the world in which we live.

God's questions to Job are, as Chesterton points out, 'a sort of psalm or rhapsody of the sense of wonder ... Instead of proving to Job that it is an explicable world, He insists that it is a much stranger world than Job ever thought it was'.[90] Many of the animals described – lions, eagles, wild asses, even the silly ostrich that stomps on its own eggs – have the quality of 'untameability', of freedom. The overall picture of the singing morning stars and animals laughing in their freedom is one of their enormous variety constituted in their freedom by a single personal Creator, who wishes his creatures to participate in some way in his own freedom.

The creation has now been shown to Job to be good, despite its often bewildering diversity. In it, some suffering is seen to be inevitable, yet understandable within God's plan. Job's response is that of awe: 'Behold, I am small; how can I refute you?' (40:3f.). Beside the presence of the creator of the entire universe, Job feels small, yet not crushed – he doesn't say, 'I am wrong'. In fact, the very restraint of his response indicates that he's not yet satisfied in the intellectual aspect of his quest, although the very presence of God to him is the vindication he's been looking for all along. Habel notes that 'Job does not retract his position, but neither does he renew his further challenge'[91] – signified by him clapping his hand to his mouth.

God's second questioning of Job

In his case against God in Chapter Thirty One, Job seemed to reject God himself, since it looked as if God had acted unjustly towards him. So God asks Job, 'Would you pervert my justice? Would you prove me wrong so that you may be in the right?'

(41:8). Central to the drama is Job's own justice, so his offence here lies in the *manner* of his self-justification. For example, his self-justificatory oath in Chapter Twenty Nine concealed an accusation against God: if Job had treated *his* servants so well, had not God mistreated *His* good servant Job most shabbily? God is not, like the 'friends', insisting that Job is unjust. Rather, he fully accepts Job's assertion of innocence, yet claims that He too is innocent.

His first answer to Job showed that the universe wasn't just rational – a mysterious harmony of mountainous yet beautiful contrasts – but beyond human reason. His second 'answer' will indicate that the divine plan can encompass not just diversity and suffering, but even chaos, and perhaps evil. This second discourse gets to the heart of Job's anguish, since it tackles the background of meaninglessness seeping into his soul. The two beasts described in Chapters Forty and Forty One, Behemoth and Leviathan, are 'mythic symbols of the forces of chaos which are overcome by Baal in Canaanite traditions, by the god Marduk in the Babylonian Enuma Elish, and by Horus in Egyptian mythology'.[92]

While God does not eliminate these chaotic beasts, he's in control of them: 'God takes [Behemoth] by the mouth with rings ... everything under the heavens is mine. Did I not silence [Leviathan's] boasting?' (40:24; 41:3f.). In these ancient Near Eastern myths, there was a struggle between the forces or gods of good and evil, of order and chaos, but Leviathan and Behemoth, 'whom I made' (40:15), are creatures of God, just as Satan is. The key question is: 'Who can take their stand before my face?' (41:10). Earlier, Job had insisted on taking a legal stand against God, but neither the monstrous Leviathan nor Job can challenge the source of their existence as equal to God.

Why is Job satisfied with God's 'answer' to his question?

In his first reply, Job was effectively silenced. Now he's convinced: 'I have heard of you by hearsay, but now my own eyes have seen You. Therefore I retract. And repent in dust and ashes' (42:5-6). Job now finds himself in the presence of God Himself and it's this encounter with God – not the mere 'hearsay' or flattened-out formalistic teaching of the 'friends', nor even the picture of creation that Elihu conveyed, with its all-powerful creator – that has finally moved Job to a much deeper relationship with God than he had before.

Job has glimpsed a creative wisdom that not only drenches the utterly diverse and contrasted existences and events of the universe with a higher meaning beyond his ken, but that can allow free beings the full play of their own created wills, including the chaos and evil often resulting from that. Yet, because Job now trusts God in a deeper way, he knows his goodness can go beyond even that chaos/evil He's permitted. When he spoke to Satan at the beginning, God trusted Job and his capacity for inner growth. And Job's inner development through the book is itself an example of God's providence for a world where the permission of chaos/evil can eventually be seen to have a meaning. Certainly by now, it's much clearer to Job that he chooses the You of God for that You's sake and not his own. This justifies God's choice of Job for his own sake, as a person who can truly love. And in His love of Job, standing for us all, all human beings are free – free to love or free not to love.

Conclusion

In his essay on Job, Chesterton speaks of 'the loneliness of God',[93] and if we remember the title of Abraham Joshua Heschel's book, *God in Search of Man: A Philosophy of Judaism*,[94] we can perhaps catch the inner essence of the Book of Job. From Chapter Thirty Eight through to Forty, we know that the nature of God is to reach out beyond himself – what's called self-transcendence – manifested in his creation of free beings. If God is utter self-transcending love, Job is utter desire for relationship with that self-transcending love. And his suffering is the extreme expression of his reaching beyond himself. He's an incarnate icon or expression of God's self-transcendence. In the end, both 'lonelinesses' meet in God's gracefulness and Job's responsive gratefulness.

On one side, everyone who has ever suffered can identify with Job and his angry questions for God. We intuitively feel he's making a case for all of us. He represents suffering humanity before God, asking why? We also found something of this in Etty Hillesum's awareness of who she was.

On the other side, haven't we often found ourselves in the position of the hapless 'friends', standing with someone in an awful situation, desperately looking for the right words of comfort, failing to find them, and misrepresenting God in our anxiety to bring consolation? Surely there are echoes of this in the questions of those denying the existence of a good God in a world of suffering. The wonder of the dramatic meditation unfolded in the Book of Job is that it includes this wide range of voices only to lift them up into the revelatory moment of encounter where everything is seen in a new light, the light, surely, of a higher love. Although love isn't directly a theme in the Book of Job, without love, it's hard to understand either Job's longing for God, or God's unshakable trust in Job's capacity for that deepest exercise of his freedom, which is the choice to love Him purely for His own sake, despite all the disasters He permits.

Harold Kushner's book[95] delineates a God who is not all-powerful, and asks, 'If God does not cause the bad things that happen to good people, and if He cannot prevent them, what good is He at all?' In his final chapter, his answer is that God has given humans the means to overcome or at least cope with suffering, and that these very sufferings bring out deeper qualities of forbearance and courage in those who suffer. He quotes Archibald MacLeish, commenting on his play, *J.B.*, a modern version of Job:

> Man depends on God for all things; God depends on man for one. Without Man's love, God does not exist as God, only as creator, and love is the one thing no one, not even God himself, can command. It is a free gift, or it is nothing. And it is most itself, most free, when it is offered in spite of suffering, of injustice, and of death.

I think some of Kushner's analyses of God – whom he sees as not perfect, because 'limited by laws of nature and human moral freedom' – could be improved on, since God isn't 'limited' by what He has freely created. Still, Rabbi Kushner is very close to Etty Hillesum in his belief that God doesn't change the structure of the universe he has created. He quotes an Auschwitz survivor from Rabbi Reeve Brenner's *The Faith and Doubt of Holocaust Survivors* who writes that, 'It never occurred to me to associate the calamity we were experiencing with God, to blame Him, or to believe Him less ... because he didn't come to our aid. God doesn't owe us that, or anything. We owe our lives to Him.' This is where Les Murray's observation that, 'The answer to that is not in/ the same world as the question ...' comes into play. Like Job, that courageous survivor has a far wider context than human evil, a context going beyond our space-time universe, where even murderous evil can be endured and transcended.

The author of the Book of Job wanted to broaden the horizons of Genesis – Adam and Eve's suffering is largely their own fault – to deal with the problem of innocent suffering. Like Isaiah's Suffering Servant, he's pointing towards a representative figure who will carry the weight of all our suffering. Pope Benedict XVI in his *Infancy Narratives* refers to Isaiah's prophecy that 'a virgin shall conceive and bear a son, and shall call his name Emmanuel' as 'a word in waiting', that couldn't be understood in its own time.[96]

For me, the whole Book of Job is a 'word in waiting', and in our final chapter we look at the suffering, death and Resurrection of someone who really was completely innocent of wrongdoing, who offers us a definitive context for all human suffering – physical, moral and spiritual – a context partly anticipated in the meditative drama played out for us in the Book of Job.

Can we ask whether there really was someone whom Chiara Lubich will call a 'world-man', someone who has faced the hardest challenge of our universal humanity, undergoing unjust suffering to the extreme of feeling abandoned by God at the point of death? Could there be someone who shockingly lives the 'incompatibility' between innocent suffering and God's goodness, because borne by One who is both Man and God?

Could it be that the Christian 'answer' to suffering is that God shares in it with us? This would go beyond Job, as Jesus goes beyond Job.

'If your God is called Why? I've been looking for Him all my life'

In the earlier chapters of this book, I drew from those who have helped me to gain a deeper insight into suffering, even though, as with Stephen Fry and Peter Singer, I sometimes disagreed with them. Now I'd like to tell you how I came across what's become for me like the light behind Georgia O'Keeffe's *Black Cross* of suffering, courtesy of the Socialist Unity Party which ran the (Communist) German Democratic Republic.

Stop Press! Priest discovers way to live the Gospel!

I was ordained in Rome not long after Vatican II. The years following the end of the Council in 1965 were a time of uncertain expectations in the Church. What was going to change following Vatican II? Were celibate priests going to be allowed to marry? Some of the very best students from my seminary class in Ireland who were ordained around the same time as me subsequently left the priesthood during the years after the Council. Pope Paul VI's restatement of the Church's teaching on contraception in

1968 was met with almost universal uncomprehending rejection in the media, in the pews, and among many moral theologians at that time. In addition, the ferment of ideas triggered by the Council and the discussion of all the issues it raised in the media, left in its wake a new uncertainty about what it meant to be a priest at all. Suddenly being a priest involved going against the current of both theological discussion and public opinion.

I was in a somewhat different situation to many of my fellow newly-ordained priests as I'd been asked to take on higher studies with a view to university teaching. This involved my going to study psychology in Leuven, Belgium. I was studying how human beings communicate and relate to one another – my topic was friendship, enmity and reconciliation – but, although I was staying in a hostel for priests, I was quite lonely. I remember on Sundays taking walks around the town hoping I might by chance meet one or other of my fellow doctoral students.

I thought I'd need a better knowledge of German for my work, and instead of taking what would have been a prohibitively expensive course in West Germany, I figured the German Democratic Republic (DDR) might have a 'Ministry for Culture', putting on German courses at least partly for propaganda reasons. Indeed they did, and applying as a PhD student in psychology, the DDR Ministry for Culture offered me what amounted to a free language course in East Berlin in August 1970.

I was treated courteously by the East Berlin border guards who presumed I was a DDR supporter. The next day I was tested at the Humboldt University on Unter den Linden to be graded for the three-week course on German. Almost all on the course were students from the East European Communist countries (the

Soviet Union, Poland, Romania, Bulgaria and Czechoslovakia), as far as I remember, all of their parents were in the Party. We were divided into nine groups and I was in group nine.

In the evening, our group would go together to the *kneipen* – pubs where you could buy a glass of wine or beer and chat for a few hours. I shared a lot with a student during this time I'll call Darina, including letting her know I was a Catholic priest. One of the highpoints of our course was a visit to Weimar, home of some of Germany's greatest writers, including Goethe and Schiller. After that visit, we all set off to our different destinations, me back to Western Europe, and most of the others towards the East. I was so out of touch with what was going on inside me, that it was only on the evening in Weimar before our last day together that I realized it wouldn't be all that easy to say goodbye to Darina.

When I got back to Leuven, I was shellshocked. Up to then I'd never admitted to myself that I'd fallen in love with her – I'd no intention of doing that with anyone – but all of a sudden it hit me, and being a talkative type, I told the few people I was close to in Leuven what had happened to me, even writing to my parents that my life had been turned upside down. We kept writing to each other every week, and early on Darina suggested I ask my spiritual director if it was right for us to relate in this way. She had been brought up in a communist family, and had been a youth leader in their Pioneer organization, but shortly before she came on this course she'd converted to Catholicism – no thanks to me, need I say.

During the year, her brother (I'll call him Peter here) tried to take his own life, and – surely with rather mixed motives – I immediately offered to go over to her country in order to help him. So the following summer, after a long train journey and complicated border crossing, I met Peter, and despite having almost no language in common, got on great with him. Darina turned out to have a wide circle of friends, and most of the time I was in her country we were together with these friends.

I was trying to do the impossible: to be a celibate priest, yet not let go of a deeply emotional relationship with her. I felt I'd only been given one life, and in that one life I'd already made a lifelong commitment. I couldn't imagine committing myself to anyone except for life, which of course I couldn't do with Darina. Even though my relationship with her was always only at the emotional level, I didn't want to admit to myself that I was betraying my vow of celibacy – at least as much as a married man would betray his spouse if he had a such a deep emotional attachment to another woman. Once I asked if I could hold her hand, and she said no, that this meant something different for a woman than for a man. Several times over the next few years she tried to help me break off the relationship, but I just wouldn't let go.

After that first visit, I returned on two more occasions. On my third visit, Darina told me of a conversation she'd had with some of her friends. They'd suggested to her that our relationship might make it hard for me to help other people carry their cross. It was as simple as that. I'd always found that everything that Darina said was both straightforward and true and so I gradually came to see more clearly that I was rationalizing my position. At last I realized I'd have to make a complete break. Her friends said we should try to work together on ending our relationship, and the fact that Darina didn't send me packing made this easier for me.

I'm in love with Jesus ... when He was an atheist

So we agreed not to write any more, unless we were at death's door. Darina then said that she was going to burn all the letters I'd sent to her. I asked her why. 'So that we don't live in the past, but towards the future.' Reluctantly, and again following her good advice, I said I'd do the same. Because my air ticket obliged me to stay a few days longer, we still had some time together. I now felt a sense of urgency. I was never going to see her again, the person who, along with my parents, had had the most influence on my life of anyone I'd met. And there were some questions I felt I had to ask her, as I might kick myself later for not doing so.

All along, since I'd met her in East Berlin, I noticed that she reached out to other people, not just me, in an extremely unselfish way. So I asked her – it shows how self-centred I must have been that this question took so long – 'Darina, what's the secret of your life?'

I was really surprised by her answer: 'I'm in love with Jesus. Especially when He was an atheist.' She explained how, brought up as an atheist, she'd always been asking why – why do people suffer, why do things go wrong in the world, what's the meaning of our life? Sharing these questions with some of her friends at university, they told her the name of their God was Why. Darina said, 'if your God is called Why? I've been looking for Him all my life!' I thought I knew my way around theology, but I'd never been told before that Jesus had been an atheist!

She explained to me what her friends had told her. When Jesus was on the cross he cried out, 'My God, my God, why have you forsaken me?' Jesus, crying out to God that God had forsaken Him! It was an astonishing idea. After all, she and her friends believed, as do I, that Jesus himself was God as well as man, so this cry on the cross, meant that in some way, at the deepest moment of his suffering he lost the experience of being the Father's Son and this made him cry out in an anguish of forsakenness.

Darina felt Jesus had identified with her own experience of being an atheist, of not having the answer to the meaning of existence any more, since for him, the meaning of his existence was to be the Son of God. Yet after that, he'd said, 'into your hands I entrust my spirit'. As she hadn't found the meaning of her existence, but only had a why, she saw that in this moment of physical forsakenness on the cross, Jesus no longer experienced unity with his Father, the Why of his life, and so underwent a spiritual forsakenness too.

This was a shock for me, but a good shock. I'd come to realize in the few days before this conversation that it was going to be hard for me to carry on my life without the relationship with her. Nor did I think God would have too much time for someone like me, who'd let him down. Yet, now Darina was showing me how the suffering I was facing in being separated from her could be lived through with him. After all, he'd suffered separation from the one he loved most, his Father, whose being he shared – 'I and the Father are one'. I'm not daring to presume my separation from Darina was remotely comparable to Jesus' separation from his Father, just that I felt he was humble enough to come down even to my level. In fact, Darina helped me every step of the way, telling me how the rays of the sun, which seem to be going apart, are really united because they're in the sun. By each of us staying on the ray God willed for us, our separation would unite us in Him.

I asked her where she'd got this striking new way of talking about a Christianity not only lived practically in a personally committed way, but in a way that lifted up and gave a positive meaning even to negative experiences. She explained how she was trying, with her friends, to live like the first Christians in the Acts of the Apostles. They shared the few goods they had, but even more, they shared their experiences of trying to live the Gospel. Then, because of Jesus' promise, 'where two or three are gathered in my name, there am I among them,' they could always have him with them – in the university, at a bus-stop or a café. Even if they were imprisoned (her country was relentlessly anti-Christian) if they put them in the same cell, they'd be sure to have Jesus with them through their mutual love.

I had a question: 'Why didn't you tell me about this before?' Darina's answer was a typically humble one: 'I felt I hadn't been living the Gospel so well, so there was no point telling you about something you hadn't seen in my life.' (But it was exactly because she *had* been living the Gospel that this question was forced out of me.) She reminded me too of something I'd completely forgotten. When we met first in East Berlin, she'd mentioned the group she'd met, but I'd said something like: 'Get out of that, those movements are really a pain in the neck!'

Then she gave a name to the spirituality she'd met, Focolare, and told me the bare bones of how it had started up in Italy in 1943 in the middle of World War II. On the way to the airport the next morning, I said that God must have a sense of humour, because if I hadn't become a priest, I never would have met her. She replied, 'no, it was through the mercy of God that we met'. A perceptive friend in Ireland kindly explained this to me later: 'You were like a concrete onion, layers and layers of cement, no one could ever reach you. Only this way could those layers be broken open.'

As we parted, Darina gave me a wooden set of Rosary beads given to her by a Lutheran friend from East Germany. I have rather poor eyesight, but to my surprise, when I was sitting in the small plane waiting for take-off I could see her on the observation deck of the airport, wearing a red plastic raincoat. I asked the young man sitting beside the window if he wouldn't mind my leaning over, and made the sign of the cross on the window. She replied by making a small sign of the cross, and just as the plane began to move, she stood out and made a big sign of the cross with her arms – which could have got her arrested.

When I got back to Dublin, I dropped into a Focolare centre that had recently opened, and through the three wonderful women there, Pina, Mary and Lieta, met the community of people in Dublin (including Eddie McCaffrey and his mother Margaret) who were trying to live out Jesus' prayer, 'that all may be one.' I'd already learned from Darina that this unity can only be arrived at by identifying with the suffering-love Jesus showed when he experienced being forsaken by his Father. That was how Chiara Lubich understood that he achieved, on principle, the unity he prayed for in his great prayer for unity. A shorthand summary of this practical way of sharing in Jesus' experience is called 'living Jesus Forsaken'.

To end this narration, I'm delighted to say that Darina married a man who deeply shared her ideals, and they've raised three wonderful children, now all grown up.

Only later did I fully grasp how deeply selfish and irresponsible I'd been, and how I could have ruined Darina's life. Thank God her own unerring commitment to the Christian message in a hostile environment helped her to carry on and make a good life for herself and later her family. I'm deeply grateful to her and to God for all I learned from her, which I think changed my own life very much for the better.

Chiara Lubich's understanding of Jesus forsaken

Let's go back to where Darina got her discovery of the centrality of the experience of Jesus Forsaken. During the bombing of Trent in 1943, a young schoolteacher, Chiara Lubich and a group of young women in Trent, North Italy, had seen all their earlier ambitions – for her, study of philosophy; for others, a fiancé and marriage, careers in medicine, art, and so on – destroyed by the war. Chiara, and then her friends, found an ideal that couldn't be destroyed: God-Love. They realized everything else was 'vanity of vanities'. One of them, Dori Zamboni, was sick, and when the priest who had brought her Holy Communion was leaving the flat where some of them lived, he asked Chiara: 'what was the moment of Christ's greatest suffering?' She wasn't sure and said, 'Maybe when he was in the Garden of Gethsemane.' He replied, 'No, it was when He cried out, "My God, my God, why have you forsaken me?"'

In a talk to young people in 1972, Chiara Lubich called that experience of Jesus a 'divine atomic explosion'. She asked:

Is there a kind of world-man who's ... felt in himself this terrible tsunami (*maremoto*) menacing all that was thought up to now to be beyond question? Is there someone who's felt his fate is completely meaningless, forsaken by Truth itself, leaving him totally confused? Is there a world-man who's been able to overcome this terrible trial, paying the price of a new world he's found in himself and given rise to in others? Yes, he exists. But we immediately grasp that this man couldn't only be a man but the *Man* – that is, Jesus Forsaken ... On the cross, close to physical death and in the mystical death of his forsakenness, Jesus is aware of the collapse of his humanity ... and at the high point of that collapse, the Father mysteriously allows him to doubt – as if in Him the presence of God is totally eclipsed. Because of this he cries out, 'My God, my God, why have you forsaken me?' (Mt 27:46)[97]

Chiara realized that if they'd committed themselves to God-Love, then it would have to be to him in the moment he showed that love the most – when he felt he was abandoned by his Father. But he'd still gone on to say: 'Into your hands I commend my spirit.' So to reach the Risen Jesus, and to realize the unity he'd prayed for, they'd have to take the same way he took, through his forsakenness on the cross.[98]

In the final few days we'd had together, Darina explained how Jesus showed us the way to unity with his Father by losing the experience of that unity. I'm under no illusions that the suffering I went through when 'losing' Darina – a relationship I shouldn't have begun in the first place – was in the same league as the far greater physical and moral sufferings many have to go through. But what she showed me has also helped many others to live their own sufferings, great or small, in a way that gives those sufferings meaning. Simone Weil reaches for the same reality when she says: 'the greatness of Christianity comes from the fact that it doesn't seek a supernatural remedy for suffering, but rather a supernatural use for suffering.'[99] Albert Camus, even though an atheist, surely has the same intimation when he comments in *The Rebel*:

> The night on Golgotha is so important in the history of man only because, in its shadow, the divinity abandoned its traditional privileges and drank to the last drop, despair included, the agony of death. This is the explanation of the *lama sabachthani* and the heartrending doubt of Christ in agony. The agony would have been mild if it had been alleviated by hopes of eternity. For God to be a man, he must despair.

And four years later in his 1955 Athens address entitled 'Lecture on the Future of Tragedy', Camus returns to this theme:

> Perhaps there has been only one Christian tragedy in history. It was celebrated on Golgotha during one imperceptible instant, at the moment of the 'My God, my God, why hast thou forsaken me?' This fleeting doubt, and this doubt alone, consecrated the ambiguity of a tragic situation. Afterwards the divinity of Christ was never again called into doubt. The Mass, which gives a daily consecration to this divinity, is the real form which religious theatre takes in the West. It is not invention, but repetition.[100]

Hide and Seek, or call Him by name

Chiara Lubich also developed a foolproof way of re-living Jesus Forsaken in the most ordinary as well as the most extraordinary sufferings that she called, after the children's game, 'hide and seek'. We've already come across examples of extraordinary suffering in Eddie McCaffery's life in the introduction and in

Chiara Badano's story in Chapter Three, suffering transformed in both instances by being lived in the light of Jesus Forsaken.

For Chiara Lubich, loving Jesus Forsaken was like a game of hide and seek because 'behind' each suffering, there's a chance to discover Jesus hidden there as the One who loves us the most. Because Jesus chooses to be there for us, not magically to remove the suffering, but to be with us and for us in it, disguised by or hiding behind each suffering that comes our way. Believing he is really waiting to be with me in each suffering I have to undergo, I can give the suffering a name. That name will always be a name for him in his moment of greatest suffering. What I have to try to do in loving that negative situation is to find him 'hiding' behind whatever the name for that suffering is. And since in his forsakenness, he identified with every kind of suffering, he's 'in' my suffering too. By loving it, I'm loving him in his forsakenness. Then he's with me, I'm not alone in the suffering anymore. This is something we have to try to live for a while before we understand what it means and the startling but substantive and transfigurative difference it makes to us in suffering.

It doesn't mean that the suffering goes away, but because I've found Jesus there, my suffering is part of his suffering, it's not quite such an impossible burden to bear. Not only the Mass, but each moment of whatever suffering comes our way is a moment when we relive the tragedy of the forsaken Jesus. And, of course, in the phrase J. R. R. Tolkien coined in his 1947 essay 'On Fairy Stories', the final act of the tragedy is not a catastrophe, but what he called a 'eucatastrophe', a surprise turning of the tables so that everything works out in the end, and that, Christians believe, is the Resurrection.

If lived well, it's a way of loving Jesus Forsaken for his own sake, not making him an instrument, or just for putting ourselves at ease, but loving him as he deserves to be loved. And the way to love him for his own sake is this: to call him by name. Chiara used to show this by picking out negative words in the dictionary and showing how each one could be a new name for Jesus Forsaken. Since this is such a practical exercise, I'll conclude by giving a few I can easily remember, all with the 'name' that Jesus was 'hiding' behind, who we can discover if we look for him in the suffering with love.

Helpless

Just before it fell to the Viet Cong during the Vietnam War, Saigon found itself with a new archbishop, Nguyen Van Thuan, at the helm. He spent thirteen years in so-called 're-education camps', which included nine years in solitary confinement.[101]

> The hardest thing … was that I began to feel helpless – my plans, my efforts, my activities were all for nothing. This 'practical helplessness' describes my condition for thirteen years. I wanted to do so many things, to serve my people, but I could not. Then I came to think about Jesus on the cross: that he was immobilized, he could neither preach nor administer any sacraments – he too, was 'helpless'. Still, it was from there that he performed his greatest deed: he redeemed us sinners. Thanks to his help, I have never regretted my destiny.

Empty Hands

A German priest I know well had for many years worked for the hierarchy on various important jobs. But a few years ago it suddenly hit him that it was all worth nothing, there wasn't any love in all he'd been doing. He came to see that he was coming to God with empty hands, that he really had nothing to offer. Then he realized – that was the experience of Jesus, too. He too, when he cried out ... had empty hands. Yet with love, he showed that having empty hands didn't matter.

Why without an answer

Dori Zamboni was one of Chiara Lubich's first companions, the one who was sick when the priest called with Holy Communion and asked Chiara when Jesus suffered the most. Sometime in 1974, Dori was in a Brussels hospital. The side effects of her treatment left her feeling very depressed, and the rather grim hospital surroundings added to it. A patient in the same ward was dying and having a very disturbed night. Dori prayed for her, but felt her own life was a waste of time, even to the point of doubting whether she believed in God anymore. But still she tried to see just what name she could call this suffering. A new name for Jesus Forsaken occurred to her then, since her depression never lifted, and there was no light coming through the clouds. That when Jesus cried out on the cross, unlike earlier moments in his life, there was no answer from the Father. His 'Why?' was a why-without-an-answer. Dori realized she was living that why-without-an-answer with him, as he was with her.

Broken bones

In 2001, I had been reading in the Harper Library at the University of Chicago about how monkeys communicate. I guess God spotted a proud thought creeping in: 'at least I'm smarter than that lot.' So, on the way out, I slipped and broke my ankle in three places. While I was waiting for six hours in the emergency department, I looked up and saw the crosses made by the tiles in the ceiling – even though the University of Chicago Hospital had no explicit religious symbols, the place was full of these crosses.

I felt I wasn't alone, and was being allowed to share a bit in His cross (even though later my friend, Joe, kindly suggested I re-read Ps 34 [33]:20 and John 19:33, where it's quite clear Jesus' legs weren't broken!). Then a group of very new interns had to yank at my leg three different times to get it into shape. I didn't complain because in a way, I was already trying to live those broken bones. I actually heard the doctor in charge when he came up to them telling them they should have given me some painkillers. When they were finished, I thanked them, and one of them said, 'I wish everyone took it like you did.' It sounds odd, I know, but as I look back on my life from the vantage point of my mid-seventies, I realise that I've never been happier than when I was in hospital – leg, kidney problems, stroke or aspirin-induced ulcer notwithstanding – because only in dire straits are you incentivized to seek out the One who loves you the most, Jesus Forsaken, and if you look for him, you'll find him when you call him by name.

What about our sins?

One of my favourite reflections of Chiara Lubich is an unpublished one called 'The Divine Comedy' – her slightly less tragic version of our participation in Camus' 'Christian tragedy'. There she lists a series of negative experiences, each being one Jesus Forsaken had: darkness, not living in the truth, even 'sin' – not that Jesus, who we're told in the Gospel is like us in all things but sin, could ever have sinned. Still, St Paul says he became sin for us (2 Cor 5:21; Gal 3:13); he felt that total estrangement from the Father more than any sinner did. Chiara advises us to try to cut the time to zero between our becoming aware we've done wrong and our snapping back into doing the right thing. She urges us to go beyond the sin by straightaway loving others concretely – a practical version of what Catholics call 'an act of perfect contrition'.

Jesus as an atheist

To return to what I learned from Darina, here are some thoughts of Chiara Lubich on the relevance of loving Jesus Forsaken in order to improve dialogue with our atheist brothers and sisters, including Stephen Fry and Peter Singer – a dialogue which, as we've seen with Albert Camus, has already begun:

> Turning our thoughts back to our brothers and sisters who profess no religious faith ... We need to present them with a sign, an emblem in which Christ seems to be nothing but a man. And that his how he appears in his forsakenness. Furthermore, they need to meet Christians who love them as much as they

are able, if one may say so, to experience like Jesus forsaken the loss of God for the sake of others – Christians who ... know how to become, as Paul says, 'as one outside the law of God' (1 Cor 9:21) ... Gradually these brothers and sisters of ours will begin to appreciate such simple and whole people. Appreciation leads to conversation, conversation to communion ... Jesus in his forsakenness is their sign and symbol, because ... for them he made himself *atheism*.[102]

AFTERWORD: LASSANA BATHILY
'Jews, Christians, Muslims – we're all brothers'

Over the past twenty years or so, the international news headlines in the media have been dominated by appalling acts of terrorism. We all remember where we were on the day the planes were flown into the Twin Towers in New York, resulting in huge loss of life.

I have looked at several examples of suffering in this book, from fatal illness to horrific atrocities. And we've seen how people with very different viewpoints have drawn on reason and religion in different ways in their struggle to see how to live with suffering.

Here I turn my attention to the contemporary world and demonstrate how, awful as they are, we must not become anaesthetized by these terrible events.[103] We need to begin to look for ways to go beyond the outrages to see if we can throw some light on why they happen: to try to ascend to the height from where, in the heart of God, Fr Mourad, Rabbi Sacks and Imam Warith Deen Mohammed, see beyond our differences to what Chiara Lubich calls 'the pre-existing bond' uniting all of us. But I'll start with my own memory of the New York 9/11 attacks.

What I said at Mass on the Sunday after 9/11

On 11 September 2001, I was on sabbatical doing some research in the wonderful University of Chicago libraries. On that Tuesday, I was taking my usual morning stroll from St Thomas Apostle rectory where I was based, to the Regenstein Library. I noticed people on the street listening to other people's car radios as the first news of the attack on the Twin Towers was unfolding. Only when I got back home that evening did I watch (for the first and only time) the unbearable footage of bodies falling from the Twin Towers, and the full horror of what had happened became clear to me. Here's what I said to the packed congregation at Mass the following Sunday in St Thomas Apostle:

Today was to be a day of prayer for the work of catechesis – but nothing will communicate better our belief to others than the way we live the present terrible crisis. And during a week in which it may have seemed that God had abandoned America, there were two feast days, the Exaltation of the Cross and Our Lady of Sorrows, that gave that abandonment a thin ray of light and of hope.

Over the last few days, trying like all of you to make sense of what happened, I remembered a meditation by Chiara Lubich. Writing about the 'Why have you forsaken me?' of Jesus on the cross, and the desolation of Mary standing beside him, she said they were like twin towers reaching up to heaven, each unable to be in touch with the other. To fully endure all the separations human beings would ever have to undergo, especially the thousands of separations of last Tuesday's victims, it seemed that both of them had to experience on their own the separation from the one they loved the most.

I'd like to make the rest of what I say be a prayer with you to them:

Jesus and Mary, may your Twin Towers of suffering and love, reaching up to the Father, transform the ruined New York Twin Towers into anguished symbols – of humanity reaching up to God and of God reaching down to humanity.

Both of you, Jesus and Mary, went through the terrible loss called by some the Dark Night of God. You, Jesus, in your humanity, felt the loss of your Father, God. And you, Mary, mother of God, felt the loss of your Son, God and man. You were both united in losing everything, not only on earth, but it seemed, also in heaven. Because you both, in that moment, lost contact with the person you loved the most; we pray you to be present in the utter aloneness of body and of spirit that the victims, their families, their rescuers and support workers went through and are going through.

In losing contact with the one you loved the most, nothing seemed to make sense anymore. Jesus, in your moment of greatest forsakenness, you heard no voice from heaven, saying, 'This is my beloved Son in whom I am well pleased.' For you, Mary, there was no explanation, only what seemed a painful brush-off, when your Son seemed to be cutting himself off from you, when he told you that now, John was your son.
So for both of you, your Why? was a Why-Without-an-Answer. That's another reason we ask you to be close to the victims of last Tuesday, and to their loved ones. Saint

Paul speaks of evil as the mystery of iniquity since it cannot be explained away or excused by anything. Jesus and Mary, please help the survivors and those closest to the victims to live your Why-Without-an-Answer with you.

And please help us, all of us in America and around the world who feel what happened to you also happened to us, to try to live your Why-Without-an-Answer too. So that by doing that, we too may grow into living Twin Towers, by being Jesus the forsaken one, and Mary, the desolated one.

How can that help, how can living your abandonment point in the direction of being an answer to the thousands and millions of Whys-Without-an-Answer the victims asked, and those closest to them, and all of us are still asking?

How can that double loss – of relationship with the ones we love the most, and of the meaning that flows into our lives because of that – be overcome?

Those who were able, sometimes at great risk to themselves, used those last moments to phone their husbands and wives, saying that despite oncoming death, they still loved them and their families, and always would.

We can suggest, with the certainty of our faith, that the courageous love that united those victims to those they loved can never die. We can say that the God prefigured in today's Gospel as the ever-merciful and suffering Father, that God would not be God, would not be Love without end, if God's love were less than their human love. We believe in your bodily resurrection,

Jesus, and in your assumption, body and soul into heaven, Mary. Which is why we beg you to bring about, one day, the resurrection of those now torn bodies. And we ask you that one day their now utterly bereft loved ones will see them again in glory, not just in spirit, but in their risen bodies, and in your company, dear Risen Jesus, dear Mary Assumed into heaven. Hear our prayers today that the grieving hundreds of thousands of their loved families and friends, will see the beloved faces of the victims again, will look with their own eyes into their shining eyes, will hold their warm hands in theirs, will hear their dear voices with their own ears, will be reunited in paradise with them forever.

Help the grieving to understand that those conversations that seemed broken off are not broken off, that those words they would have wished to say, they can still say. Because in our eternal Twin Towers between God and humanity, in you, Jesus forsaken and Risen, in you, Mary, desolated and assumed into heaven, we pray that the victims are alive forever, that they are always open to the prayers and requests of those they love, and eager to help them.

We pray that, in the one mystical Body of the Risen Christ, all gaps in conversation between victims and their loved ones may be reconnected. Especially, Jesus, we pray that our celebration just now of your new covenant of love, your eucharistic sacrifice, may help to bring all of the victims, without exception, into your heavenly kingdom, and some peace to the thousands of bereaved. We ask this, along with you, Mary, through your Son, Jesus Christ Our Lord. Amen.

For the many thousands of other innocent victims of terrorism in our times, that question I asked echoes and re-echoes: how can that double loss, of relationship with the ones we love the most, and of the meaning that flows into our lives because of that, be overcome? Here's one exceptional answer.

I forgave my tormentor even as he was whipping me

Father Jacques Mourad was head of Mar Elian monastery and of Al-Qaryatayn parish, near Palmyra, Syria. He was abducted by members of Islamic State on 21 May 2015 and kept prisoner for almost five months. Threatened with beheading several times if he didn't convert to Islam, whipped and subjected to a mock execution, Fr Mourad's prison experience was certainly a 'way of the cross':

'The first week was the hardest: after being held for several days in a car, I was taken on Pentecost Sunday to Raqqa. I lived those first days in captivity, torn between fear and anger.' On the eighth day, a man dressed in black came into his cell. Father Jacques asked why he'd been abducted. His jailer said:

'Consider it a spiritual retreat.' 'From then on, my prayer, my days took on a meaning. I felt that through him, it was the Lord who sent me these words. Through prayer, I was able to regain my peace. It was May, the month of Mary. We began to recite the Rosary ... My relationship with the Virgin was renewed by it. Saint Teresa of Ávila's prayer, 'Let nothing disturb you, nothing frighten you', also kept me going. Charles de Foucauld's prayer helped me abandon myself into the hands of the Lord, well aware I'd no choice', as it seemed 'either I converted to Islam, or I'd be beheaded.'

Through prayer, the Psalms, I found a sense of peace that never left me. I remembered Christ's words: 'Bless those who curse you, pray for those who persecute you.' I was happy to be able to live out these words. It's no small thing to be able to live the Gospel, especially those difficult verses, which were previously only theoretical. I started to feel compassion for my captors.

Suddenly, on the twenty-third day, his captors reappeared, and he was whipped for thirty minutes.

I was in physical pain, but deep down inside I was at peace. I'd great comfort knowing I was sharing something of Christ's suffering. I forgave my tormentor even as he was whipping me. Later, I remembered the verse where the Lord says that his strength is manifested in our weakness. I experienced my greatest fear a little later when a man armed with a knife entered our cell. I felt the blade of his knife on my neck, and thought the countdown for my execution had begun. In my fright, I recommended myself to God's mercy. But it was only a horrifying sham.

On 4 August, Islamic State seized Al Qaryatayn, taking the whole Christian population hostage. A few days later a Saudi sheikh entered the Syrian priest's cell: 'Are you Baba Jacques? Come! Some Christians from Qaryatayn have been bothering us about you!' I thought that I was being taken away to be executed. Sitting in a van, we drove for four hours straight. Beyond Palmyra we took a mountain path to a building secured by a large iron door. When it was opened, what did I see? The whole population of Qaryatayn, amazed to see me. For them it was an extraordinary moment of joy.

Twenty days later, on 1 September, we were brought back to Qaryatayn, free, but we were forbidden to leave the village. A collective religious contract was signed: we were now under their protection upon payment of a special tax. A few days later, after the death of one of my parishioners, we went to the cemetery, near the Monastery of Mar Elian. Only then did I notice it'd been razed to the ground. Curiously, I didn't react. I understood Mar Elian had sacrificed his convent and his cemetery in order to save us.

Today I still feel for my captors the same feeling I had for them when I was their prisoner: compassion. This feeling comes from my contemplation of God's gaze on them, despite their violence, which is the same one that he has for every man: a gaze of pure Mercy, without any desire for revenge.[104]

The voice and living witness of exceptional people like Fr Jacques shows us one way to go beyond the suffering. The overwhelming truth and goodness of their witness shows up the moral and spiritual emptiness of the ideals driving their tormentors. Faced with the innate dignity of their victims, the terrorists' actions are unmasked as offensive to reason as much as to religion, and contrary to the nature of the God addressed in every surah, bar one, of the Qur'an as 'the Merciful, the Compassionate.' Still we also need to go beyond this suffering in another way, by understanding why these terrorists do what they do. This Why also needs an answer. One exploration of that issue was carried out by Pope Benedict XVI.

POPE BENEDICT XVI: *'Whoever would lead someone to faith needs to be able to speak well and to reason properly, without violence and threats'*[105]

Pope Benedict XVI gave his famous lecture in the University of Regensburg in Germany in 2006. It's a short talk, just sixty-three paragraphs in total, but it raises pertinent questions about the relationship between religion and violence in contemporary society: is the use of violence to compel people to adhere to a religion acceptable? Is it in keeping with the dignity of human persons? Is it in keeping with the will of God?

Whether it's permissible to use violence to force people into religious belief isn't a new issue, and Pope Benedict shows this very clearly by examining the interaction between the Christian Byzantine Emperor Manuel II Palaiologos and an educated Persian Muslim in AD 1391:

> The emperor must have known that surah 2,256 reads: 'There is no compulsion in religion.' According to some of the experts, this is probably one of the surahs of the early period, when Mohammad was still powerless and under threat. But naturally the emperor also knew the instructions, developed later and recorded in the Qur'an, concerning holy war.

The emperor asked, 'Is it reasonable, or does God will, to spread one's religion by violence?' The issue is the deliberate choice of violent means as a proper way to propagate a religion, together with a theological justification for doing so. Within the Qur'an there are two different answers to the question of the use of violence in religion, one that says 'no', one that says 'yes'. The current Islamist turmoil in the world is caused by those in Islam who answer 'yes' to this question.

What Pope Benedict was concerned with was the basis of the claim that it is reasonable to compel people to belong to one's religion by violence:

> The emperor ... goes on to explain ... why spreading the faith through violence is something unreasonable. Violence is incompatible with the nature of God and the nature of the soul. 'God,' he says, 'is not pleased by blood – and not acting reasonably is contrary to God's nature. Faith is born of the soul, not the body. Whoever would lead someone to faith needs to be able to speak well and to reason properly, without violence and threats ... To convince a reasonable soul, you do not need a strong arm, or weapons of any kind, or any other means of threatening a person with death ...' The decisive statement in this argument against violent conversion is this: not to act in accordance with reason is contrary to God's nature ... For the emperor ... shaped by Greek philosophy, this statement is self-evident. But for Muslim teaching, God is absolutely transcendent. His will is not bound up with any of our categories, even that of reason.

The emperor uses the word 'logos' for reason, the same word St John uses when he opens his Gospel with, 'In the beginning was the Word (Logos)'. When we put reason aside, emphasize will *without* reason, and then apply that to our action in the world, we can say our God justifies *any* behaviour, even when it goes completely *against* reason. 'From the very heart of Christian faith and, at the same time, the heart of Greek thought now joined to faith, Manuel II was able to say: 'Not to act "with logos" is contrary to God's nature.'[106]

However, we know that at times Christians too of all denominations have used force to compel others to accept their beliefs. However belatedly in history, on 7 December 1965, the Second Vatican Council issued its affirmation of the right of religious freedom of conscience, the Declaration on Religious Liberty (*Dignitatis humanae*). Below is its key statement, in paragraph two:

> The Vatican Council declares that the human person has a right to religious freedom. Freedom of this kind means that all men should be immune from coercion on the part of individuals, social groups and every human power so that, within due limits, nobody is forced to act against his convictions in religious matters in private or public, alone or in associations with others. The Council further declares that the right of religious freedom is based on the very dignity of the human person as known through the revealed word of God and by reason itself. This right of the human person to religious freedom must be given such recognition in the constitutional order of society as will make it a civil right.

Following this groundbreaking declaration, successive popes have offered formal apologies for past grave situations where this right was not respected by Catholics.[107]

Despite what were seen as ideologically orchestrated violent protests to the Regensburg lecture, Pope Benedict's words were met with a courteous response from Islamic scholars, which developed into the Catholic–Muslim Forum. The theme of the first forum in November 2008 was 'Love of God, Love of Neighbour'; the second in November 2011, held in Jordan, discussed 'Reason,

Faith and the Human Person.' The third forum, in Rome, on 'Working Together to Serve Others' in November 2014 – was held on the eighth anniversary of the one hundred and thirty eight Muslim Scholars' letter in 2007 to Catholic leaders after the Regensburg lecture. The Muslim delegates were from the Middle East, Africa, Europe, Asia and North and South America. All the delegates, Muslim and Catholic, 'unanimously condemned acts of terrorism, oppression, violence against innocent persons, persecution, desecration of sacred places, and the destruction of cultural heritage'.[108]

Muslim appeals for moderation

There have been many Muslim efforts to address the violence of Al-Qaeda, the Taliban, and Islamic State factions, moves that are vital in staving off mass radicalization. Two years before Pope Benedict's Regensburg lecture, there emerged what's called the *Amman Declaration* or *Message*, a statement eventually signed by more then five hundred leading Islamic scholars. They maintained that the tenets of Islam bear witness to noble principles and values such as the fundamental goodness of humanity. The foundation of these principles is the 'oneness' of the human species, and that people are equal in rights and obligations. The *Declaration* continues:

> Together, these are principles that provide common ground for the followers of religions and [different] groups of people. That is because the origin of divine religions is one, and Muslims believe in all Messengers of God and do not differentiate between any of them. Denying the message of any one of them is a deviation

from Islam. This establishes a wide platform for the believers of [different] religions to meet the other upon common ground, for the service of human society, without encroaching upon creedal distinctions or upon intellectual freedom.[109]

Barely a month later, thirty eight Islamic scholars debated in an open letter the contents of Pope Benedict's Regensburg lecture. One commentator called them 'unquestionably among Islam's most senior clerics and prominent scholars'.[110] They included Mohammed-Ali Taskhiri from Iran, the Grand Mufti of Egypt and dignitaries from Russia, Bosnia, Istanbul and Oman.

Moreover, the 24 September 2014 open letter to Islamic State signed by one hundred and twenty prominent Islamic scholars, used the Qur'an, along with accepted sayings of Mohammad and classical Sunni writings, to refute Islamic State interpretations of those same writings.[111]

A Muslim encounter with Focolare[112]

In May 1997, Chiara Lubich was invited by Imam Warith Deen Mohammed, leader of the American Society of Muslims, and an international president of the World Conference of Religions for Peace, to speak at Malcolm Shabazz Mosque in Harlem, New York. In her address to the overspill congregation of three thousand people, including over thirty imams from all over the US, she quoted from a revered saying of Mohammad to great applause: 'none of you is a believer until you want for your brother what you want for yourself'.

She gave an example of the kind of cooperation that has happened between Christians and Muslims:

For example, in Solingen, Germany, right after a Turkish family had been killed as a result of racism, the young Muslims and Christians – who'd been living their different faiths in the light of the Focolare spirituality of unity in a spirit of mutual respect and friendliness – organised an event to promote reconciliation. In those circumstances, it was a courageous act that went against the current. They organized a big concert for peace in the centre of the town with the participation of young people of various ethnic groups who gave a witness of unity. It was a decisive contribution towards restoring peace to people's hearts.

She finished by saying: 'All that is left for us to do now is to hope that today will really be a milestone, the beginning of a new era, in which we all love one another. Let us love one another and work together. A Christian saint, John of the Cross, once said: "The world belongs to those who love it and who can give the best proof of their love." And that's something all of us can do together.'

Then Imam Mohammed spoke, saying that: it is a great day for us. History is being made here in Harlem, New York, in Malcolm Shabazz's Mosque … We welcome this great lady and we will keep her in our hearts.' Soon after, Chiara Lubich said: 'The God whom we all love and believe in had created a bond among us and, in a way, had made us one. Undoubtedly he was present there while Imam Mohammed and I were speaking, filling everyone with joy, a joy we could hardly contain. Many were moved. God left no doubt in our minds that we are all his children, all sisters and brothers.'[113]

I heard Rashida, one of the women belonging to Warith Deen Mohammed's American Society of Muslims, share an experience at a Focolare community meeting in Chicago in 2002. She was at a party to mark her retirement from where she'd worked. One man there was someone she hadn't gotten on with for years. She remembered something she'd learned from members of the Focolare Movement – that we must be the first to love. Rashida felt she shouldn't lose this opportunity. She went over and put her arms around the man. He was very moved, and the years of not talking were forgotten in that moment.

During the 9 January 2015 attack on a Paris kosher foodstore, the courage and quick thinking of Lassana Bathily, a young Muslim immigrant from Mali, saved the lives of fifteen Jewish patrons. Bathily helped customers to hide in the basement, phoning the police and showing them how to enter from the basement (the gunman was on the first floor). Rabbi Sacks notes that 'Commended for his courage, [Lassana] replied: "We are all brothers. It's not a question of Jews, Christians or Muslims. We were all in the same boat, we had to help each other to get out of the crisis."'

And on 13 November 2015 during the Islamic State onslaught on Paris, Safer, a Muslim of Algerian origin, was working at the Cosa Nostra bar. At great risk to himself, during a lull in the firing, he ran out from cover, picked up two wounded women and rushed them downstairs: 'I sat with them and tried to stop the bleeding. As we were downstairs, we could hear the gunfire continuing above. It was terrifying. As frightening as it was, they had in fact escaped much worse. When we came out we saw bodies in the street. So many were injured.' Despite the dark tragedy surrounding them, the actions of brave people like Lassana and Safer highlight the common humanity of Muslims, Jews and Christians alike.[114]

It's actions like these that prove to me too that it's possible for us all, Christians, Jews and Muslims, Buddhists and Hindus, people of every religion or none, all united by our shared moral convictions, to understand that, after all, we do belong to the one human family and that we too can act like Rashida, Lassana and Safer. Despite differences in belief and doctrine, it's always possible, with good will, for us to live together – there's an 'ecumenism of life' as Chiara Lubich called it, where we look each other in the face and find God smiling back at us.

In her address to the first international meeting for Muslim friends of the Focolare Movement in Castel Gandolfo outside Rome in May 1992, Chiara Lubich quoted the thirteenth-century Muslim poet Rumi, 'God has predestined us eternally for love'. She then followed with the words of the great medieval Sufi scholar Ibn Arabi:

> My beloved, love me!
> Love only me, love me with a true heart!
> No one is closer to you than I.
> Others love you for themselves.
> But I love you only for you …

She concluded with:

> And then, after having loved him, we will also love our brothers and sisters, as God asks of us when he says: 'Love your neighbour as yourself' (Lev 19:18) and we will love one another as Jesus teaches in his principal commandment: 'Just as I have loved you, you also should love one another' (Jn 13:34). And through this love we will contribute to building universal brotherhood in the one Father God …[115]

Isn't this at least a first step on the path we need to follow, the seed of a hope for an answer to the suffering facing us from Islamist terrorism? Surely it's possible for Christians, Jews and Muslims to put to one side polemic, nationalism and petty power struggles in order to live together as one and feel what Chiara herself felt towards her Muslim brethren: 'when I am with them I feel as if I am among brothers and sisters. I attribute this to our common faith in God. I feel that there is a pre-existing bond that was there already. And it is God, the same God that we both love.'[116]

END NOTES

1. Archibald MacLeish, *J.B., A Play in Verse* (Boston: Houghton Mifflin, 1986), p. 11.

2. Stephen Fry's answer is easily available on: http://www.joe.ie/entertainment/video-gay-byrne-asks-staunch-atheist-stephen-fry-about-god-the-reactions-from-both-are-incredible/483016. The podcast of my interview with Marian Finucane may still be accessible on RTÉ Radio 1, Marian Finucane, 31 January 2015.

3. If this book doesn't meet your need, as it's a mixture of the intellectual (because of the intellectual challenge made by Stephen Fry and Peter Singer and others who quite rightly ask similar questions) and the practical (because it's only at the level of life that we can try to work through our suffering), there are surely many other books around. Two I have to hand are: Rea McDonnell SSND, *Why God: A Glimpse into the Mystery of Suffering* (Hyde Park, NY: New City Press, 2002) and Ronda Chervin's *Avoiding Bitterness in Suffering: How Our Heroes in Faith Found Peace amid Sorrow* (Manchester, NH: Sophia Institute Press, 2015).

4. An extract from *Dear Pope Francis: The Pope Answers Letters from Children Around the World*, Antonio Spadaro SJ and Tom McGrath eds. (Dublin: Messenger Publications, 2016), pp. 64–5.

5. Bishop Robert Barron, 'Stephen Fry, Job, and the Cross of Jesus', in *Word On Fire*, 10 February 2015.

6. As I write this, my friend Fr John McNerney, outgoing head chaplain at University College Dublin, spoke in his parting words about just this shared feeling, which bonded Irish student survivors of a terrible 2015 accident in Berkeley, California, with those around them: 'The Berkeley tragedy will always be etched on my soul. I remember one day going around the hospitals in the aftermath and visiting the injured. I was in a hospital room with one of the families. A nurse (Kim) came in to care for one of the injured students. She asked if she could share an experience with us. She explained how she had suffered in her own life and how along the way some people were not very helpful to her. She ended up feeling treated like an object. But she then turned to the injured student and said "Look I see in you a very positive attitude, a real

determination to live this awful event well. Believe it or not, you'll grow on the inside in all of this, you'll grow as a human person, you'll grow on the inside ..." What she said was very moving for us all' (2 March 2016).

7. *Irish Times* Religious Affairs Correspondent Patsy McGarry gives a full account of Stephen Fry's remarks in his *Irish Times* piece, 'Stephen Fry tells Gay Byrne: God is a "maniac, totally selfish"' (2 February 2015).

8. I wrote a summary as 'Conversation between Peter Singer and Brendan Purcell on "The role of reason in faith and unbelief"', in *The Melbourne Anglican*, 6 May 2012.

9. Quoted by Eric Voegelin in his *Hitler and the Germans*, Volume 31 of *The Collected Works of Eric Voegelin*, Detlev Clemens and Brendan Purcell, eds. and trans. (Columbia, MO: University of Missouri Press, 1999), p. 88.

10. Quoted by Eric Voegelin in his *Anamnesis: On the Theory of History and Politics*, M. J. Hanak, trans., David Walsh, ed., Volume 6 of *The Collected Words of Eric Voegelin* (Columbia, MO: University of Missouri Press, 2002), pp. 370–1.

11. An early biographer writes of him: 'He was above all things a great giver; and he cared chiefly for the best kind of giving which is called thanksgiving. If another great man wrote a grammar of assent, he may well be said to have written a grammar of gratitude. He understood down to its very depths the theory of thanks; and its depths are a bottomless abyss.' Maisie Ward, *Gilbert Keith Chesterton* (London: Sheed and Ward, 1945), p. 410.

12. Gilbert Keith Chesterton, *Autobiography* (London: Hutchinson, 1937), p. 334.

13. *Etty: The Letters and Diaries of Etty Hillesum 1941–1943*, Klaas A. D. Smelik, ed., Arnold J. Pomerans, trans. (Grand Rapids: Eerdmans, 2002), p. 640.

14. Peter Singer, 'Good God? Religious people are still unable to provide a satisfying answer to the age-old question of why God allows suffering', *The Guardian*, Saturday, 17 May 2008.

15. I've explored this more technically, drawing on Bernard Lonergan's notion of emergent probability, in *From Big Bang to Big Mystery: Human Origins in the light of Creation and Evolution* (Dublin: Veritas, 2011).

16. *Rare Earth* (New York: Copernicus, 2000), p. 220, quoted in *The Privileged Planet: How Our Place in the Cosmos is Designed for Discovery*, Guillermo Gonzalez and Jay W. Richards (Washington DC: Regnery, 2004), p. 45.

17. Gonzalez and Richards *The Privileged Planet*, p. 55.

18. Taking consciousness as the defining standard of worth, Singer, who considers infanticide of a child up to at least two years old as justifiable in the case of serious

handicap, writes that 'There will surely be nonhuman animals whose lives, by any standard, are more valuable than the lives of some humans. A chimpanzee, a dog, or pig, for instance, will have a higher degree of self-awareness and a greater capacity for meaningful relations with others than a severely retarded infant or someone in a state of advanced senility.' *Animal Liberation: A New Ethics for Our Treatment of Animals* (London: Jonathan Cape, 1976), p. 19.

19.   For a more detailed discussion of the development of evolutionary thinking within the context of divine creation see my *From Big Bang to Big Mystery*, Chapter 4.

20.   See Patsy McGarry, 'Stephen Fry tells Gay Byrne: God is a "maniac, totally selfish"', in *The Irish Times*, 2 February 2015.

21.   Damian Thompson, 'Sir James MacMillan mourns the little granddaughter who brought "cosmic love" to his family,' *Spectator,* 21 January 2016.

22.   I'll use the word 'Presence' to refer to what philosopher Eric Voegelin speaks of as the presence of God to each human being and to all humankind. See his *Hitler and the Germans*, Volume 31 of *The Collected Works of Eric Voegelin*, Detlev Clemens and Brendan Purcell, eds. and trans. (Columbia, MO: University of Missouri Press, 1999), pp. 70–4; 204–12.

23.   James MacMillan, 'Blessed by a Little Angel', *Catholic Herald*, 22 January 2016.

24.   Fyodor Dostoevsky, *The Brothers Karamazov*, Richard Pevear and Larissa Volokhonsky, trans. (New York: Farrar, Straus & Giroux, 1990) pp. 242–3, 245.

25.   Fyodor Dostoevksy, *Notes from Underground* and *The Double*, Jessie Coulson, trans. (London: Penguin, 2003), p. 119. The first part of *Notes from Underground* (1864) is Dostoevsky's nineteenth century diagnosis of what C. S. Lewis in the twentieth century called *The Abolition of Man* – the widespread reduction in intellectual circles of human beings to the level of animals or even of chemicals. The second part illustrates the awful inadequacy of the Underground Man's reaction against this, which is to proclaim his utter freedom, not merely from being merely a animal, but from any limits whatever on his desires.

26.   Martin Buber, *I and Thou* (Edinburgh: T & T Clark, 1966), pp. 67–8.

27.   Flannery O'Connor, 'Introduction to a Memoir of Mary Ann', in her *Mystery and Manners: Occasional Prose* (Farrar, Straus & Giroux, New York, 2000), pp. 226–7.

28.   *Summa Theologiae*, I, q.19, a. 9 ad 3. There's a full discussion in Bernard Lonergan, *Grace and Freedom: Operative Grace in the Thought of St Thomas*

Aquinas, Vol. I of *The Collected Works of Bernard Lonergan*, Frederick E. Crowe and Robert M. Doran, eds. (Toronto: University of Toronto Press, 2000), pp. 328–48.

29. Inge Scholl, *The White Rose: Munich 1942–1943* (Middletown, CN: Wesleyan University Press, 1983), p. 58.

30. David Walsh, *The Growth of the Liberal Soul* (Columbia, MO: University of Missouri Press, 1997), pp. 230, 231–2, with Mochulsky quoted on p. 349, n. 15. I'm grateful to Matthew Leslie and his excellent 2015 Master's thesis at the University of Notre Dame (Australia), 'Freedom in the Philosophy of David Walsh' for clarifying Dostoevsky's discussion for me.

31. Voegelin, *Hitler and the Germans*, p. 87; see also pp. 27 and 96.

32. Aleksandr Solzhenitsyn, *The Gulag Archipelago 1: 1918–1956, Parts I and II* (London: Collins, 1974), p. 168.

33. David Walsh, *The Modern Philosophical Revolution: The Luminosity of Existence* (New York: Cambridge University Press, 2008), p. 463.

34. Quoted in Elisabeth Young-Bruehl, *Hannah Arendt: For the Love of the World* (New Haven: Yale University Press, 1982), p. 368.

35. Hans Jonas, *Le concept de Dieu après Auschwitz: Une voix juive* (Paris: Payot & Rivages, 1994), pp. 39–40.

36. William Clifford, 'The Ethics of Belief', *Contemporary Review*, 1877. Reprinted in *Lectures and Essays* (1879). Presently in print in William Kingdon Clifford, *The Ethics of Belief and Other Essays* (Prometheus Books, 1999).

37. Fyodor Dostoevsky, *The Brothers Karamazov*, p. 589.

38. Brendan Purcell, 'Six reasons why I think Stephen Fry is wrong', *The Irish Catholic*, 2 February 2015.

39. Focolare, the Italian for 'fireside', was the name given to a group which began in Trent, Northern Italy, in 1943, whose ideal was to bring about the fulfilment of Jesus' prayer in Chapter 17 of St John's Gospel 'That all may be one.' After the war, it spread throughout Europe and the rest of the world, with members from Catholic, Anglican, Reformed and Orthodox Christians. From the 1970s it has attracted Jewish, Muslim, Hindu and Buddhist members, along with those of non-religious convictions. On Chiara Lubich and the Focolare Movement, see Jim Gallagher, *A Woman's Work: Chiara Lubich* (Hyde Park, NY: New City Press, 2003); Armando Torno, *Chiara Lubich: A Biography*, Bill Hartnett, trans. (Hyde Park, NY: New City Press, 2012).

40. The story of Eddie's life has been written by an old friend of his, Fr Maurus Green OSB, *The Vanishing Root: Eddie McCaffrey's Story* (London: New City, 1994).

41. V. E. Frankl, *Man's Search for Meaning* (Boston: Beacon Press, 2006), p. 109. Its original 1946 title was *Trotzdem Ja Zum Leben Sagen: Ein Psychologe Erlebt das Konzentrationslager* [*Saying Yes to Life in Spite of Everything: A Psychologist Experiences the Concentration Camp*] which gave me the heading for this chapter.

42. Brendan Purcell, 'Long Night's Journey into Eternal Day', in *Treasures of Irish Christianity: People and Places, Images and Texts*, Salvador Ryan and Brendan Leahy, eds. (Dublin: Veritas, 2012), pp. 269–71 at p. 270.

43. Brendan Purcell, 'Finnegan's Waiting for God?' in *Treasures of Irish Christianity: A People of the Word*, Salvador Ryan and Brendan Leahy, eds. (Dublin: Veritas, 2013), pp. 237–9 at p. 239.

44. Viktor Frankl, *Man's Search for Meaning*, pp. 48–9.

45. Mariagrazia Baroni and Jacopo Lubich, *Chiara Luce: Life Love Light* (Supplement to number 3/2011 of *Città Nuova*), p. 5.

46. Zanzucchi, *Chiara Luce: A Life Lived to the Full* (London: New City, 2014), p. 28.

47. Franz Coriasco, *Dai tetti in giù: Chiara Luce Badano raccontata dal basso* (Rome: Città Nuova, 2011), p. 91.

48. Ibid., p. 96.

49. Ibid., p.73.

50. See Baroni and Lubich, *Chiara Luce*, p. 17.

51. Zanzucchi, *Chiara Luce*, p.22.

52. The bar-café was owned by the parents of one of Chiara Luce's closest friends, Giuliana Robbiano. See Zanzucchi, *Chiara Luce*, p 32.

53. Baroni and Lubich, *Chiara Luce*, p. 29.

54. Ibid., p. 19.

55. Zanzucchi, *Chiara Luce*, p. 38.

56. Ibid., p. 52.

57. Baroni and Lubich, *Chiara Luce*, p. 42.

58. Ibid., p. 40.

59. Coriasco, *Dai tetti in giù*, pp. 76–7.

60. Ibid., p. 91.

61. Ibid., p. 88.

62. Zanzucchi, *Chiara Luce*, p. 49.

63. Coriasco, *Dai tetti in giù*, p. 90.

64. Ibid., p. 43.

65. Zanzucchi, *Chiara Luce*, p. 39.

66. All the page references here – preceded when possible by their date – are to

Etty: The Letters and Diaries of Etty Hillesum 1941–1943, Klaas A. D. Smelik, ed., Arnold J. Pomerans, trans. (Grand Rapids: Eerdmans, 2002).

67.   The editors of the *Letters and Diaries* note that 'The women who were put to work [in Auschwitz] were given such heavy tasks that their "life expectancy" was estimated at a maximum of two months' (783). Etty was transported on 7 September 1943 and died on 30 November 1943. For her biography, see Klaas A. D. Smelik, 'A Short Biography of Etty Hillesum (1914–1943)', in *Spirituality in the Writings of Etty Hillesum: Proceedings of the Etty Hillesum Conference at Ghent University*, November 2008, Klaas A.D. Smelik, Ria van den Brandt, and Meins G. S. Coetsier, eds. (Leiden: Brill, 2010) – here referred to as *Proceedings*, pp. 21–8.

68.   Aleksandr Solzhenitsyn, *The Gulag Archipelago 1: An Experiment in Literary Investigation* (London: Fontana, 1974), p. 168.

69.   See Wil van den Bercken, 'Etty Hillesum's Russian Vocation and Spiritual Relationship to Dostoevsky', in *Proceedings*, pp. 147–71 at p. 168.

70.   'God is weak and powerless in the world, and that is exactly the way, the only way, in which God can be with us and help us … Man's religiosity makes him look in his distress to the power of God in the world … The Bible, however, directs us to the powerlessness and suffering of God; only a suffering God can help.' Dietrich Bonhoeffer, *Letters and Papers from Prison*, Eberhard Bethge, ed. (New York: Touchstone, 1997), p. 343.

71.   Van den Bercken, 'Etty Hillesum's Russian Vocation and Spiritual Relationship to Dostoevsky', p. 163.

72.   For a full exploration of Etty's inner dialogue with God, see Meins Coetsier, *Etty Hillesum and the Flow of Presence: A Voegelinian Analysis* (Columbia, MO: University of Missouri Press, 2008); also Klaas A. D. Smelik, 'Etty Hillesum and her God', in *Proceedings*, pp. 75–102.

73.   J. G. Gaarlandt, ed., *Het verstoorde leven: Dagboek van Etty Hillesum 1941–1943* (Haarlem: De Haan, 1981).

74.   Her brother Jaap's connections resulted in her being appointed to the Dutch Jewish Council, which, at least temporarily, exempted her from incarceration. See Klaas A. D. Smelik, 'A Short Biography of Etty Hillesum (1914–1943)', p. 26.

75.   The editors of *The Letters and Diaries* note that 'Hes Hijmans offered her a place to hide but Etty refused it' (710). Then 'Werner Sterzenbach … tried to persuade Etty to go into hiding because he hoped to use her literary talents in the service of the active Resistance. Etty refused because … she did not want to desert her parents and she believed it was her task to help people in

the Westerbork camp' (756). They further record how Klaas Smelik (Klaas A. D. Smelik's father) and his daughter planned to kidnap Etty and hide her in their house in Hilversum. Yet another time, Smelik recalls grabbing her and trying to convince her of the danger: 'She looked at me very strangely and said, "You don't understand me". I replied: "No, I don't understand what on earth you're up to. Why don't you stay here, you fool!" Then she said: "I want to share the destiny of my people". When she said that, I knew there was no hope. She would never come to us.' The editors continue: 'Others also offered Etty a hiding place, but she steadfastly refused this' (761).

76. I'm using Klaas A. D. Smelik's translation in his 'Etty Hillesum and Her God', *Proceedings*, p. 98.

77. Quoted by the editors in the *Letters and Diaries*, p. 762.

78. And Van den Bercken comments that 'Here we have a significant term "harmony", which Ivan Karamazov used in his rebellion against God, as well as two other characteristic Dostoevskian expressions: "meekness" and "real love". "Real love" is contrasted with the "abstract love" of mankind which Ivan Karamazov has, but which is only an argument he uses in order to reproach God for lack of love of mankind', in 'Etty Hillesum's Russian Vocation and Spiritual Relationship to Dostoevsky,' taken from p. 169.

79. Harold S. Kushner, *When Bad Things Happen to Good People* (New York: Anchor Books, 2004). There are also chapters on Job in, for example, Hans S. Reinders, *Disability, Providence and Ethics: Bridging Gaps, Transforming Lives* (Waco, TX: Baylor University Press, 2014) and J. Todd Billings, *Rejoicing and Lament: Wrestling with Incurable Cancer and Life in Christ* (Grand Rapids, MI: Brazos Press, 2015). Fabrice Hadjadj has written a hilariously ironic modern setting of Job with his play *Job ou la torture par les amis* (Paris: Salvator, 2014).

80. Les Murray, 'The Knockdown Question', in *New Collected Poems* (Manchester: Carcanet, 2003), p. 538.

81. Hadjadj updates Job's losses, with Satan listing them as Job losing his business due to the financial crash brought about by speculators. His wife has left him for his human affairs manager, and his children died in the tragic Macumba Night Club fire, started by a partly extinguished Lucky Strike. Then he was stricken by lupus erythematosus – an autoimmune inflammatory disease causing scaly red patches on the skin, especially on the face. Finally he was accused of abuse of power, embezzlement, and cruelty towards a young female intern – to the point that his reputation is trashed in the media (Hadjadj, *Job*, p. 12).

82. Norman C. Habel, *The Book of Job* (London: SCM Press, 1985), p. 111.

83. Language reminding me of Bertie Wooster's 'and he meant it to sting' – Fry and Singer show surprising animosity towards a being that for them doesn't exist – or do they somehow think He does? Voldemort never got it so hard.

84. New York abstract expressionist painter Barnett Newman captures this intrinsic dialogicality in his painting, *Covenant* (1949), with two vertical 'zips' as he called them: black for Adam, meaning man as earthen, and gold for God. Yet in the painting, the human's mortal 'I' and God's immortal 'I' are parallel, in some sense equal. And the blood red background to the zips indicates the depth of suffering underlying this pledged faithfulness of God to each human 'you' and of us to God.

85. Hadjadj, *Job*, p. 31.

86. Emmanuel Levinas, *Etica e infinito* (Rome: Città Nuova, 1984), p. 101.

87. Emmanuel Levinas, *Totalité et infini: essai sur l'extériorité* (The Hague: Nijhoff, 1968), p. 190.

88. Habel, *The Book of Job*, p. 306.

89. Gilbert K. Chesterton, 'The Book of Job', in *G.K.C. as M.C.* (London: Methuen, 1929), p. 44f.

90. Ibid., p. 48.

91. Habel, *The Book of Job*, p. 549.

92. Ibid., p. 557.

93. Chesterton, *G.K.C. as M.C.*, p. 39.

94. Abraham Heschel, *God in Search of Man: A Philosophy of Judaism* (New York: Harper & Row, 1955).

95. Kushner, *When Bad Things Happen to Good People* (New York: Anchor Books, 2004), pp. 152, 160, 147, 95.

96. Joseph Ratzinger/Pope Benedict XVI, *Jesus of Nazareth: The Infancy Narratives* (New York: Image, 2012), p. 50.

97. In *Colloqui con i gen* (Rome: Città Nuova, 1999), pp. 75 and 81. Despite being well behind the Iron Curtain, Darina was up to date on what Chiara had been telling these young people the previous year.

98. There's a full account of this in Chiara Lubich, *The Cry*, Julian Stead OSB and Jerry Hearne, trans. (London: New City, 2001). See also *Chiara Lubich: Essential Writings: Spirituality, Dialogue, Culture*, Michel Vandeleene, Thomas Masters and Callan Slipper, eds. (Hyde Park, NY: New City Press, 2007), pp. 16–26; 88–97.

99. Simone Weil, *Gravity and Grace* (London: Routledge, 2002), p. 81.

100. Albert Camus, *The Rebel* (New York: Vintage, 1992), p. 32; 'Lecture Given in Athens on the Future of Tragedy', in Albert Camus, *Selected Essays and Notebooks*, Philip Thody, ed. (London: Penguin, 1963), pp. 197–8.

101. See Francis Xavier Nguyen Van Thuan, *The Road of Hope: A Gospel from Prison* (Hyde Park, NY: New City Press, 2013). These 1,001 extracts are taken from Van Thuan's letters from prison, secretly written on the back of smuggled-in calendar pages and circulated among Vietnamese Christians and Buddhists during the worst years of religious persecution after the war in Vietnam.

102. Lubich, *The Cry*, pp. 114–15.

103. 'Islamist' is the word best used for the terrorism we're speaking about here – not 'Islamic', which is the adjective describing the beliefs and action of the more than a billion Muslims who have nothing to do with the Islamists.

104. Arthur Herlin, 'Father Mourad: Defeating ISIS within a Cell of Prayer', *Aleteia* 6 December 2015.

105. Rabbi Jonathan Sachs would agree: '*Religion is at its best when it relies on strength of argument and example. It is at its worst when it seeks to impose truth by force* [his own italics].' See his outstanding *Not in God's Name: Confronting Religious Violence* (New York: Schocken Books, 2015), p. 234.

106. Pope Benedict XVI, 'Faith, Reason and the University: Memories and Reflections', in University of Regensburg, 12 September 2006.

107. Around two dozen such apologies were brought together and published by Luigi Accatoli in *When A Pope Asks Forgiveness: The Mea Culpa's of John Paul II*, Jordan Aumann OP (New York: Alba House, 1998).

108. Zenit Staff, 'Final Statement of Third Meeting of Catholic-Muslim Forum', Zenit.org, 13 November 2014.

109. Easily available on the internet. The two occurrences of 'different' in square brackets are in the text itself.

110. John F. Cullinan, 'Instead of Burning Effigies: A group of Muslim scholars composes a noteworthy response to the pope's Regensburg speech', in *National Review Online*, 30 October 2006.

111. Ayman S. Ibrahim, 'Muslim Scholars vs ISIS: Is the Open Letter to the Islamic State Really Enough?' in *First Things*, 3 October 2014.

112. In *Not in God's Name*, p. 2, Rabbi Jonathan Sachs speaks of the need for 'a theology of the Other, which is what I offer in this book'. I'd suggest developing that theology of the Other in the direction of a theology of communion between ourselves and every Other.

113. There's a full account in Piero Coda, *Nella Moschea di Malcolm X: Con Chiara Lubich negli Stati Uniti e in Messico* (Rome: Città Nuova, 1997), pp. 13–28;

Under 'interreligious dialogue' the archives of *Living City Magazine* has various articles on W. D. Mohammed and on the ongoing dialogue with his American Society of Muslims.

114. 'Muslim Employee Saved Lives in Attack on Paris Kosher Supermarket,' in *Haaretz*, 10 January 2015; Jonathan Sachs gives twenty as the number of Jewish customers Lassana saved in *Not in God's Name*, p. 25; James Longman, BBC News, 1 November 2015.

115. Lubich, *Essential Writings*, pp. 348–9.

116. Ibid., Chiara Lubich answering questions from Muslims, p. 354.